Transfer of Title Concerning Movables Part IV –
Eigentumsübertragung an beweglichen Sachen in Europa Teil IV

Salzburger Studien zum Europäischen Privatrecht

Herausgegeben von Prof. DDr. J. Michael Rainer

Band 21

PETER LANG
Frankfurt am Main · Berlin · Bern · Bruxelles · New York · Oxford · Wien

Arthur Salomons

Transfer of Title Concerning Movables Part IV – Eigentumsübertragung an beweglichen Sachen in Europa Teil IV

National Report: The Netherlands

Edited by Johannes Michael Rainer –
Herausgegeben von Johannes Michael Rainer

PETER LANG
Europäischer Verlag der Wissenschaften

Bibliographic Information published by Die Deutsche Bibliothek
Die Deutsche Bibliothek lists this publication in the Deutsche Nationalbibliografie; detailed bibliographic data is available in the internet at <http://dnb.ddb.de>.

The appearance of this book was made possible by the Austrian Science Fund FWF.

ISSN 1435-6090
ISBN 3-631-53948-7
US-ISBN 0-8204-7726-5

www.peterlang.de

Table of Contents

Part I: Basic information on property law

1. Notion of ownership and other property rights

1.1. Sedis materiae

The rules regarding property law are to be found in Books 3 and 5 of the *Burgerlijk Wetboek*, both of which were enacted in the year 1992, when the central part of a new Civil Code (in Dutch: *Burgerlijk Wetboek*, henceforward to be abbreviated as: BW) was enacted.[1] The BW (or at least the part which deals with patrimonial law, Book 3-8) is characterized by a hierarchical structure, both between the Books and within each Book, from general to specific ("layered structure"). This explains why the rules on transfer in general are found in Book 3, while ownership is dealt with in Book 5: a transfer applies to all kinds of property (in Dutch: *goederen*, which comprises both of patrimonial rights and corporeal things, see art. 3:1 BW), while the notion of ownership is restricted to things (corporeal objects, *Sachen*, in Dutch: *zaken*, see for a definition art. 3:2 BW).[2] The rules on dismembered rights which can only apply to things are also to be found in Book 5 (servitudes, emphyteusis (or: long-term lease), the right of superficies and apartment rights), while the dismembered rights which can apply to all property (again: both things and patrimonial rights) are dealt with in Book 3. Book 5 is titled Real Rights, Book 3 Patrimonial Law in General.

1.2. General basics

Dutch patrimonial law (as is the case in most, if not all, European countries) is subdivided into property law, inheritance law and the law of obligations. The distinction between proprietary rights (rights in rem) and contractual rights

---

[1] Book 1 (Law of Persons and Family Law) was introduced in 1970, Book 2 (Legal Persons) in 1976, Book 8 (Law of transport) in 1991, Books 3 (Patrimonial law in general), 5 (Real Rights), 6 (General part of the law of obligations) and Title 7.1 (Sale and exchange) in 1992, Book 4 (Law of Succession) in 2003. Since 1992, several Titles of Book 7 (Special Contracts) have been introduced, but the project is not yet completed (e.g. Title 7.17 on Insurance is still lacking). The *Travaux préparatoires* (in Dutch: *Parlementaire* geschiedenis) have been published by Kluwer Publishers in Deventer; I will refer to these by *Parl.Gesch.*, followed by the number of the Book of the BW.

[2] The Dutch term *goederen* covers movable and immovable tangible objects (*zaken*) and personal and real rights that represent a certain monetary value (*vermogensrechten*). Art. 3:1 BW provides: 'Property (*goederen)* is comprised of all things and of all patrimonial rights.' Art. 3:2 BW: 'Things (*zaken)* are corporeal objects susceptible of human control.' Art. 3:6 BW: 'Patrimonial rights (*vermogensrechten)* are those which, either separately or together with another right, are transferable; rights which are intended to procure a material benefit to their holder; or rights which have been acquired in exchange for actual or expected material benefit.'

(obligations) was established by a famous ruling of the Dutch Supreme Court, the *Hoge Raad der Nederlanden* (henceforward: *Hoge Raad*, abr. HR) from 1905.[3] In this case, the *Hoge Raad* ruled that contractual obligations with regard to an immovable (in this case the obligation to construct a road on one's land) do not bind the person to whom the immovable is sold and transferred; after this transfer, the person obliged to perform is the one who has entered into the contract, not the new landowner.[4] From 1905 onwards, therefore, Dutch patrimonial law has been characterized by a sharp division between rights in rem with absolute effect (including *droit de suite*), and personal obligations which bind only the original parties involved. In later developments the distinction has lost its initial sharpness via the introduction of new exceptions,[5] but as a basic rule it still remains valid.
A further characteristic of Dutch property law is its adherence to the principle of a numerus clausus of property rights. The numerus clauses rule can be found in art. 3:81 § 1 BW:[6]

> *A person who is entitled to an independent and transferable right, may, within the limits of that right, establish the dismembered rights* ***recognized by law****. He may also transfer his right subject to such a dismembered right, provided that he respects the rules pertaining to both the transfer of such property and the establishment of such a dismembered right.*

I will return to this provision below (in § 1.3 under c and § 1.4.3). Nevertheless, its importance is not to be exaggerated. Even if it - correctly - provides that Dutch property law does not acknowledge absolute rights other than ownership and the dismembered rights which have found their way into the BW, the Dutch patrimonial law enacted in 1992 is characterised by a fundamental openness: [7] there is room for (the acknowledgement of) new legal concepts as long as they meet two criteria: they have to fit into the system of law and be in keeping with

---

[3] HR 3-3-1905, *W.* 1905, no. 8191 (*Blaauboer-Berlips*).

[4] As the new landowner is not obliged to perform, and the former landowner is no longer able to perform, the original performance (to construct a road) will be converted into an obligation to pay damages.

[5] The most noteworthy of these is to be found in art. 6:252 BW which rules that a contract may stipulate that the obligation of one of the parties to tolerate or not to do something in respect of his registered property will be transferred to the persons who will acquire the property by way of particular title, and that the stipulation may also bind those who will acquire a right to use the property from the title-holder. For this stipulation to have effect, a deed must be drawn up by a notary of the contract between the parties, followed by its entry in the public registers.

[6] See for a translation of the Dutch Civil Code of 1992: P.P.C. Haanappel and E. MacKaay, *Nieuw Nederlands Burgerlijk Wetboek. Het vermogensrecht* (Deventer 1990).

[7] This view was introduced by the authoritative W. Snijders, until 1998 vice president of the Dutch Supreme Court and until 1995 Government Commissioner appointed to complete the new Burgerlijk Wetboek.

the rights which are recognized by law. In this light, Dutch property law should not be described as 'closed' but as 'half open':[8]
Besides the numerus clausus rule, there are several other general principles of Dutch property law. I will distinguish six of them (publicity, exclusivity, priority, droit de suite, absolutism, protection of good faith).

1.2.1. Publicity

Of vital importance is the principle of **publicity**[9]. As property rights have absolute effect (see below), they must be "noticeable". The importance of publicity is best demonstrated in the provisions regarding transfer (one could even say that for most categories of goods the requirement of publicity focuses not on the question whether one *owns* a certain object, but on the question whether one has *acquired* the object. The only exception is registered property, of which third persons can at any time find out not only by who and to whom the object was transferred in the past, but also who is the present owner of the object). Publicity concerning transfer will be dealt with below in greater detail, when I describe the different forms of transfer. Two examples may suffice here:

- **movables** are delivered by giving possession to the acquirer (art. 3:90 § 1 BW). This can be done *sine manu*[10] (art. 3:115 under a-c; constitutum possessorium, brevi manu, longa manu), but when the alienator and acquirer choose for delivery through constitutum possessorium, they have to take into account that our legislator has "discriminated" against this form of delivery in two ways:

  a) a delivery constitutum possessorium can only be performed by a possessor, not by a detentor. This follows from the fact that art. 3:115 BW speaks of "transfer" of possession; only a possessor is capable of a *transfer* of possession, whereas a detentor can only "give" possession (see art. 90 § 1 BW). The rule can also be deduced from art. 3:111 BW:

  A person who has begun detention for another pursuant to a juridical relationship continues to do so under the same title, so long as no change is apparent in his title which results either from an act by the person for whom he holds or from the latter's right having been contested.

  This provision is an adaptation of the well-known maxim *sibi causam possessionis mutare potest* (*Dig*. 41.V.2.1).

---

[8] See in particular W. Snijders, "De openheid van het vermogensrecht. Van syndicaatszekerheden, domeinnamen en nieuwe contractsvormen", in: *Onderneming en 10 jaar nieuw Burgerlijk Recht* (Deventer 2002), p. 27-58.
[9] See Snijders/Rank-Berenschot, *Goederenrecht* (3rd ed., Deventer 2001), nos. 80 and 81.
[10] See Pitlo-Reehuis, *Goederenrecht* (11th ed., Deventer 2001), nos. 226-242.

b) Art. 3:90 § 2 BW provides:

Delivery of a thing which remains in the hands of the alienator has no effect with respect to a third person who has a prior right to the thing, until the time when the thing has come into the hands of the acquirer, unless the third person has consented to the alienation.

The effect of this provision is that delivery by constitutum possessorium (obviously: by a possessor, as detentor cannot deliver by constitutum possessorium) does not have any effect towards the owner and other title-holders as long as the object has not yet come into the hands of the acquirer. These two rules combined (artt. 3:111 and 3:90 § 2 BW) have the purpose and effect of discriminating delivery by constitutum possessorium, exactly because this form of delivery lacks publicity. Formulated differently: with regard to movables, Dutch property law favours publicized transfer over non-publicized transfer. It does not, however, prohibit non-publicized transfer: it acknowledges that delivery by constitutum possessorium cannot be missed for economic reasons.

- **Assignment**[11] also requires some form of publicity, as follows from art. 3:94 § 1 BW:

  In cases other than those provided for in the preceding article, rights to be exercised against one or more specifically determined persons are delivered by means of a deed intended for that purpose and notice thereof given by the alienator or acquirer to those persons.

Notification of the debtor is an essential element of the assignment: the transfer does not take effect until the notification is performed. This requirement, however, is controversial, and in October 2004 (because of the unexpected advance of factoring and securitisation) a new paragraph has been added to art. 3:94 in which an alternative form of assignment is laid down. This new form of assignment (labelled "silent assignment" in Dutch literature) does not require notification to take effect: both an authentic deed and a registered deed under private writing will suffice. This is not the place to elaborate on this development in detail. For our present purpose it is important to note that the introduction of silent assignment (as an alternative to "public assignment") implies a concession to the principle of publicity for the benefit of those involved in the new financial instrument of securitisation. See on the principle of publicity also below, § 5.4.1.

[11] Pitlo-Reehuis, *Goederenrecht*, no. 255-290.

1.2.2. Exclusivity

Property rights are characterized by **exclusivity**[12], as can be demonstrated by the provision regarding the right of the owner to use his property (art. 5:1 § 2 BW):

> *To the exclusion of everybody else, the owner is free to use the thing provided that this use not be in violation of the rights of others and that it respect the limitations based upon statutory rules and rules of unwritten law.*

The principle of exclusivity is expressed with the words "to the exclusion of everybody else." Most authors hold that exclusivity is not so much a characteristic of ownership, but of all proprietary rights.[13]

1.2.3. Priority

In case of a collision between two property rights the issue is decided by the principle of **priority;** the oldest property right is stronger than the younger one (*droit de preference, prior tempore, potior iure).* The principle of priority can be regarded as an consequence van de *nemo-plus* rule.[14]

1.2.4. Droit de suite

Property rights are characterized by the notion of ***droit de suite***: the title-holder is allowed to follow (*suivre*) and claim his property regardless of in whose hands it may be. The same applies to the person entitled to a dismembered right. Of course, priority and droit de suite are closely connected and both principles are faced with the same limitations and exceptions.

1.2.5. Absolutism

Yet another way of describing the same phenomenon is found in the principle of **absolutism**: property rights have absolute effect (from the Latin *absolutus:* dissolved, detached) and can be invoked against whoever is in possession of the object.

---

[12] Snijders/Rank-Berenschot, *Goederenrecht*, no. 34-35.

[13] I have challenged this view with regard to security rights (pledge and hypothec), which in my opinion should not be considered as exclusive rights; see A.F. Salomons, 'Exclusiviteit van eigendom: hoeveel solidariteit kan van een eigenaar verwacht worden?', in: *Privaatrecht tussen autonomie en solidariteit*. Bundel Amsterdams Instituut voor Privaatrecht 1 (M.W. Hesselink-C.E. du Perron-A.F. Salomons eds.; The Hague 2003), pp. 241-260.

[14] *Nemo plus iuris ad alium transferre potest, quam ipse haberet* (Dig. 50.17.54, Ulpianus) (no one is able to transer more rights than he himself owns).

1.2.6. Protection of good faith

The last three principles (priority, droit de suite, absolutism) are subject to important exceptions. The principal exception is the **protection of good faith**[15], which in itself can be regarded as a principle. The Dutch civil code contains a well-elaborated set of provisions regarding this third party protection. The most important provisions – which will be dealt with below in greater detail - are 3:86 (movables), 3:88 (immovables and claims) and 3:36 (general protection of the third party acting in good faith). At this point, it suffices to say that this principle, protecting the acquirer who did not know nor ought to have known that his acquisition was encumbered with the proprietary right of someone else, is closely connected to the principle of publicity: there is no need and room for the protection of someone who was able to know the proprietary rights of others, because they were "published" in the prescribed form. Cf. in this context art. 3:11 BW:

> *Where good faith of a person is required to produce a juridical effect, such person is not acting in good faith if he knew the facts or the law to which his good faith must relate or if, in the given circumstances, he should know them. Impossibility to inquire does not prevent the person, who had good reasons to be in doubt, from being considered as someone who should know the facts or the law.*

1.3. Notion of ownership

As stated above, in Dutch property law only *corporeal* objects can be the object of ownership. This follows from the definition of ownership in art. 5:1 § 1 BW (*"Ownership is the most comprehensive right which a person can have in a thing")* and the definition of things in art. 3:2 (*„Things are corporeal objects susceptible of human control")*.
Furthermore, we see that only objects susceptible to human control can be owned. Water in the sea and the air around us cannot be the object of ownership, until it is put in, e.g., a jar or a bottle.
With regard to the rights connected to ownership, the Dutch legislator has rejected the (modern, Anglo-Saxon) bundle of rights theory in favour of the (ancient, continental) view that the notion of ownership is undetermined and therefore it is impossible to enumerate all rights (powers) of the owner. Nevertheless, the three most important rights connected to ownership have indeed been enumerated in the

---

[15] Pitlo-Reehuis, *Goederenrecht*, nos. 153-156.

BW: the right to use the object, the right to revendicate it, and the right to dispose of it:

a) the right to **use** the object (and its limitations) is to be found in art. 5:1 § 2 BW:

   To the exclusion of everybody else, the owner is free to use the thing provided that this use not be in violation of the rights of others and that it respect the limitations based upon statutory rules and rules of unwritten law.

b) the right to **revendicate** the object is to be found in art. 5:2 BW:

   The owner of a thing is entitled to revendicate it from any person who detains it without right.

   This right ends, of course, as soon as the object is acquired by another person, e.g. by prescription[16] or by acquisition by a third-acquirer in good faith.[17]

c) the right to dispose of the object (better: of his right with regard to the object) is, in principle,[18] the exclusive right of the owner. This, however, is not explicitly laid down in the BW. Cf. art. 3:81 § 1, first sentence:

   A person who is entitled to an independent and transferable right, may, within the limits of that right, establish the dismembered rights recognized by law.

   This provision states that the title-holder of an object is entitled to establish dismembered rights, but not that he may also transfer the object entirely. Relevant in this context is art. 3:83:

   Ownership, dismembered rights and debts are transferable, unless this is precluded by law or by the nature of the right.

   Transferability does not imply the right to dispose of the object, as transferability relates to the object, whereas the right to dispose thereof relates to the title-holder. We will return to this provision below, in § 1.4.3.

---

[16] Art. 3:99 § 1 BW: *Rights in movable things which are not registered property and rights under documents payable to bearer and order are acquired by a possessor in good faith by uninterrupted possession for three years; other property is acquired by uninterrupted possession for ten years.* The possessor in bad faith is also entitled to acquisition through presciption, as follows from art. 3:105 § 1 BW: *A person who possesses property at the time of the completion of the prescription of the right of Action to terminate possession, acquires the property even if his possession was not in good faith.* As the revendication prescribes in 20 years (see art. 3:306 BW), the thief of a movable object becomes the owner of his loot in 20 years time. It goes without saying that this new provision, as far as I know without precedent in other countries, is rather controversial among Dutch scholars. I do not have to deal with this in more detail, because this questionnaire is concerned with transfer, not prescription.

[17] See for movables art. 3:86, for immovables and claims art. 3:88 BW (See below, § 5.1.3).

[18] I will not elaborate on the well-known exceptions of bankruptcy and attachment here.

1.4. Restrictions on ownership

The right of ownership is *in itself* not limited or restricted. This can be explained by the fact that ownership is regarded as an undetermined right: there are no limitations, until the owner starts exercising the rights that stem from his right. Therefore, we have to focus on the restrictions attached to the various rights of the owner, that is: restrictions regarding the use of the thing (§ 1.4.1.), regarding revendication (§ 1.4.2.) and regarding the right to dispose of the thing (§ 1.4.3.).

1.4.1. Restrictions regarding the use of the thing

Art. 5:1 § 2 BW provides:

> *To the exclusion of everybody else, the owner is free to use the thing provided that this use not be in violation of the rights of others and that it respect the limitations based upon statutory rules and rules of unwritten law.*

In this provision, the right of the owner to use the thing is limited in three ways:

1. the owner is obliged to respect the **rights of others**. This refers in the first place to the situation that the owner himself has established a dismembered right (e.g. usufruct or pledge) or a personal right (e.g. lease) on the object of his ownership.[19] Furthermore, the owner is not entitled to interfere with other rights or hinder their title-holders: a landowner should take the interests of neighbouring landowners into consideration and „may not cause nuisance to owners of other properties to a degree or in a fashion which is unlawful"; see art. 5:37 BW.
   This provision is *not* relevant to the situation in which the thing is transferred by the detentor to a third person and the latter is protected on the basis of his good faith; if the object were a movable (e.g.: a bike), sold by its lessee, the acquirer in good faith would be protected by art. 3:86 BW (assuming that the requirements of this provision are met). This protection is „real", which means that the acquirer becomes the owner instead of the former owner (the lessor). This implies that the former owner is no longer entitled to use or to revendicate the bike.
2. The owner is obliged to respect the **limitations based upon statutory rules.** This refers both to provisions within the BW (e.g. the aforementioned art. 5:37,

[19] This relates to the right of revendication: when, for example, a bike has been leased by the owner to a lessee for the period of six months and this period has not yet ended, the owner is obliged to honour this: he is not entitled to use the bike himself if this would violate the rights of the lessee (as will almost certainly be the case), and he is not entitled to revendicate the bike (this follows from the provision that revendication is only allowed from persons who detain the thing of an owner without right; see below).

the prohibition of hindrance), and to provisions enacted by the national legislator outside the BW. Furthermore, the rule encompasses provisions in "lower legislation", e.g. municipal or provincial ordinances. The relevant provisions usually deal with – that is: limit – the free use of objects, whether it be by the owner or not.
It must be stressed that, while ordinances may limit the free use of a thing by its owner, it has been left to the courts to decide whether ordinances may provide rules which award the right to use a thing to someone other than the owner (violation of the principle of exclusivity). Ordinances cannot take away the right of the owner to use his thing altogether, nor can they limit in any way the right of the owner to dispose of his thing.[20]

3. Finally, the owner is obliged to respect the limitations based upon **rules of unwritten law.**
In the first place, this refers to art. 6:162 BW, the general provision on **tort law**, stating that a person who commits an unlawful act toward another which can be imputed to him, must repair the damage which the other person suffers as a consequence thereof (§ 1) and that the violation of a rule of unwritten law pertaining to proper social conduct is deemed to be unlawful (§ 2).
Secondly, it refers to art. 3:13 BW, the **'prohibition on abuse'**, stating that the holder of a right may not exercise it to the extent that it is abused (§ 1), and that instances of abuse of right are the exercise of a right with the sole intention of harming another or for a purpose other than that for which it was granted; or the exercise of a right where its holder could not reasonably have decided to exercise it, given the disproportion between the interest to exercise the right and the harm caused thereby (§ 2): this provision, too, presupposes numerous rules of unwritten law pertaining to proper conduct towards others.
Thirdly, it applies to **practice** (customary law, usage). An example is to be found in art. 5:42 BW: unless the owner has consented, or the adjacent land is a public road or public water, any trees, shrubs or hedges must not be within a certain distance from the boundary of the property of another person. This distance is, for trees, two metres from the middle of the base of the tree, and half a metre for shrubs and hedges, unless a shorter distance is permitted pursuant to an ordinance or local usage. It follows that a landowner may be obliged to tolerate the presence of trees within a distance of less than two metres from the boundary of his property when local usage permits this shorter distance.

[20] See on this subject R. Meijer, 'Het eerste van vijf; de exclusiviteit van Eigendom', in; *Liber Amicorum NBW* (Arnhem-Deventer-Zwolle 1991), pp. 73-78, and *Parl.Gesch.* (Inv. Boek 3, 5 en 6), Boek 5 (Deventer 1990), p. 1004.

Finally, it applies to **unwritten rules of public law.** This is at once clear from art. 3:14 BW, stating that a right which a person has pursuant to private law, may not be exercised contrary to the written or unwritten rules of public law. Does the provision have independent significance? Yes and no. One could maintain that the provision is superfluous, next to the artt. 6:162, 3:13 and 3:14. Nevertheless, the legislator deemed it useful to enumerate the restrictions, stemming from these articles, to stress that the right of ownership does not furnish a valid defence against claims based upon unlawful Action, abuse of right or exercise of a right contrary to public law.

1.4.2. Restrictions regarding revendication

The owner's right of revendication is restricted in several ways:

- When the owner brings a revendicatory Action against a possessor (*detentor pro se*), the owner will have to prove that the possessor is not the owner; see art. 3:119.
- A revendicatory Action cannot be commenced against someone who is entitled to use the thing or otherwise is entitled to detain the thing on the basis of a personal or real right.
- When the owner has lost the thing through theft or loss, he runs the risk that this has resulted in the loss of his ownership (because of the protection of the acquirer in good faith (art. 3:86) or because the finder has fulfilled all the legal obligations and has acquired the ownership of the lost thing (after one year, on the basis of art. 5:5).
- When the finder has not acquired the ownership of the lost thing (e.g. because the loss occurred less than one year before the revendication), he may, nevertheless, be entitled to a reward. He does not have a right of retention on the lost thing, however.
- When the revendicatory Action is commenced against a possessor in good faith, art. 3:120 enumerates several restrictions, strengthened by a right of retention (§ 3):

    1. *Separated natural fruits and civil fruits which have become exigible belong to the possessor in good faith.*
    2. *The title-holder of property who claims it from a possessor in good faith or has recovered it from him is obliged to reimburse him for the costs expended on the property, as well as for the damages for which, by virtue of the rules of title 3 of Book 6, the possessor might be liable toward third persons by reason of his possession; this obligation ceases to the extent that the possessor has been indemnified by the fruits of the*

property and the other benefits which he has drawn from it. The judge may reduce the reimbursement due if full reimbursement would result in an inequitable advantage of the possessor over the title-holder.

3. *As long as a possessor in good faith has not received the reimbursement due to him, he has the right to suspend restitution of the property.*
4. *The provisions of this article also apply to a person who believes and could believe that he has lawfully acquired possession, although he knows that the acts necessary for delivery of the right have not taken place.*

A possessor who is not in good faith is obliged to restore to the owner the separated natural fruits and the civil fruits which have become exigible, without prejudice to his liability for the damage suffered by the owner and in addition to the restitution of the thing. He may claim against the owner the reimbursement of the costs which he has expended on the thing or which he has made to produce the fruits only to the extent that his claim can be based on the rules regarding unjust enrichment (art. 3:121 BW).

1.4.3. Restrictions regarding the right to dispose of the thing

With regard to the right of the owner to dispose of the thing one has to distinguish between the right to transfer the thing (better: to transfer *the ownership of* the thing) and the right to establish dismembered rights like a pledge and usufruct.
The former is dealt with in art. 3:83 BW. Ownership, dismembered rights and debts are transferable, unless this is precluded by law or by the nature of the right, while the transferability of debts can also be excluded by agreement between the creditor and debtor. Other rights are not transferable except if so provided by law. Obviously, transferability is not to be confused with the right to transfer: the former is a quality of the object, the latter a quality of the title-holder. But it goes without saying – and has not even been laid down in the code - that the right to transfer an object belongs exclusively to the owner (cases of execution by pledgee or mortgagee, bankruptcy and seizure excluded), so the limitations of transferability and the limitations of the right to transfer concur.
The right to establish a dismembered right belongs to the person "who is entitled to an independent and transferable right" (art. 3:81 § 1 BW). This implies a first restriction: when the object is not independent or not transferable, no dismembered right can be established. Two more restrictions are to be found in § 1 of the same article:

- An established dismembered right must be „within the limits" of the right on which it is established. This refers to the *nemo plus* rule. When I have established a servitude on my land, e.g. permitting my neighbour to pass over my land, and after that I grant a right of usufruct on that land to someone else, the latter is bound by the provisions of the servitude, as I am not entitled to transfer more rights than I have myself.

- The dismembered right has to be „recognized by law". This is the enactment of the *numerus clausus* rule, the status of which under present Dutch law has been described above.

1.5. Other property rights in movables

The BW acknowledges, besides ownership, four proprietary rights in movables:

- **Usufruct:**[21] gives a right to use property belonging to another and to enjoy the fruits thereof (art. 3:201).
- **Right of use and right of habitation.**[22] These two rights are more ore less variations on usufruct, which is acknowledged by the fact that, with some exceptions, the rules regarding usufruct apply *mutatis mutandis* to the right of use and the right of habitation (art. 3:226 § 1). The crucial exception is to be found in § 4 of the same article: a person having the right of use or the right of habitation cannot alienate or encumber it; nor can he allow the thing to be used or the dwelling to be inhabited by another person.[23]
- **Hypothec:**[24] is a dismembered right, established upon registered property, intended to provide recourse against the property subjected thereto for a claim for the payment of a sum of money, with preference over other creditors. Where it has been established upon other property, it is a pledge (see art. 3:227 BW).
- **Pledge:**[25] the same as a hypothec (see above), but established on property other than registered property.

None of these rights are restricted to movables, and most of them not even to things:[26] an usufruct is also possible on all other goods (art. 3:201), the rights of use and habitation are also possible on immovable things (art. 3:226), a pledge is also possible on rights payable to bearer or order, on the usufruct of such a thing or right, or on claims (in short: on all non-registered property, see art. 3:227 § 1),

[21] See Pitlo- Reehuis, *Goederenrecht*, nos. 678-705.
[22] *Ibid.* nos. 703-705.
[23] The rights of use and habitations are only possible on things and therefore ought to have been placed in Book 5 (Real Rights). Because of the close connection with usufruct, however, it has found its way into Book 3, annexed to Title 8 (Usufruct).
[24] See Pitlo-Reehuis, *Goederenrecht*, nos. 837-912.
[25] *Ibid.*, Section 14 § 3 and 4.
[26] The BW contains four other proprietary rights, all of them restricted to things and are therefore dealt with in Book 5 (Real Rights): Servitutes, Emphyteusis, the Right of Superficies and Apartment rights.

and a hypothec is possible on all registered property susceptible of transfer (art. 3:228 in conjunction with art. 3:260 BW).

The numerus clausus rule does not preclude the creation of new proprietary rights in special laws (outside the code). Indeed, this has been done in the past, for example the proprietary right of one's own grave.[27] This, however, is an exception to the rule: property law constitutes a system that is laid down in the code.

1.6. Protection of ownership and other property rights

Several types of Action are available to the owner and other title-holders against possible infringements of their rights. I will distinguish between the Action of revendication, the Action to obtain a declaratory judgement, a tort Action, and an Action arising from unjustified enrichment.

1.6.1. Revendication

The principal Action for the owner is the revendication (art. 5:2 BW): *The owner of a thing is entitled to revendicate it from any person who detains it without right.* The revendication enables the owner (and the other title-holders to whom the Action is also available; see below) to recover his property in its current condition.

It can be instituted both against the person who is in actual possession of the property (either as immediate possessor or as immediate detentor) and against the person (the mediate possessor or mediate detentor) who possesses or detains the property which is detained for him by another (see art. 3:107 BW). Example: owner A of a bike can revendicate it both from the thief B and from the person C to whom B has rented the bike. This Action against the mediate possessor or mediate detentor will not succeed, however, when the latter is not in a position to instruct the detentor to return the property.[28]

The revendication also fails when the defendant is entitled to detain the property on the basis of a legal relationship with the owner. This is the case when owner A has leased a thing or has granted usufruct on the thing to B: for the duration of these relationships, revendication by A from B is precluded.

The limitation period for revendication is 20 years (art. 3:306 BW. Before 1992 this used to be 30 years).

---

[27] Created in the Funeral Law of 1869. See Asser-Mijnssen-De Haan, *Goederenrecht* 3-I (14th ed. Deventer 2001), § 39.

[28] See Hof (= Court of appeal) Amsterdam 25–6-1947, NJ 1947, 579 and Hof Amsterdam 26-6-1947, NJ 1947, 580.

1.6.1.a. Revendication by persons other than the owner

The Action is also available for the emphyteutic holder, the superficiary and the usufructuary, who are put on a par with the owner.[29]
Indirectly, the possessor of a thing is also entitled to revendicate property on the basis of loss or disturbance: this follows from art. 3:125 § 1 BW:

> *He who has acquired possession of property can, on the basis of a subsequent loss of or disturbance in the possession, institute the same Actions against third persons to recover the property and to remove the disturbance as the title-holder of the property. Nevertheless, these Actions must be instituted within the year following the loss or disturbance.*

This short-lived revendication by the possessor will not succeed against anyone, as § 2 provides that

> *(...) the Action is rejected if the defendant has a better right than the plaintiff to the detention of the property or if he has performed the disturbing acts pursuant to a better right, unless the defendant has taken possession from the plaintiff or has disturbed his possession in a violent or surreptitious manner.*

This means that the Action will succeed against those who have no rights to the property whatsoever and against those who have obtained their possession at the expense of the former possessor: to the latter category belong the thief, the incompetent detentor and the person who has acquired the thing from someone who was not entitled to dispose of the thing.[30]
After the expiry of one year since the loss or disturbance this course of action is no longer available to the possessor, but this does not preclude him from bringing an Action on the basis of a tort claim; art. 3:125 § 3 BW.

1.6.1.b. Revendication from a possessor

As has been mentioned above (§ 1.4.2.), in the case of revendication from a possessor in good faith, art. 3:120 BW determines that the owner is obliged to reimburse him for the costs expended on the property, as well as for the damages for which the possessor might be liable toward third persons by reason of his possession. This obligation ceases to the extent that the possessor has been indemnified by the fruits of the property and the other benefits which he has drawn from it. The judge may reduce the reimbursement due if full reimbursement would result in an inequitable advantage for the possessor over the

---

[29] Asser-Davids-Mijnssen-Van Velten, *Goederenrecht* 3-II (13th ed. Deventer 1996), § 115.
[30] A.S. Hartkamp, *Compendium van het vermogensrecht volgens het nieuwe Burgerlijk Wetboek* (5th ed.; Deventer 1999), no. 119.

title-holder. As long as a possessor in good faith has not received the reimbursement due to him, he has the right to suspend restitution of the property. In the case of revendication from a possessor in *bad* faith[31], the latter is entitled to the reimbursement of costs which he has expended on the revendicated object only to the extent that his claim can be based on the rules regarding unjust enrichment (art. 3:121 BW).
The same is true (*mutatis mutandis*) for situations in which property is revendicated from a detentor: in the event that a third person claims property as the title-holder from somebody who detains it for another person, articles 3:120 and 121[32] apply to that detentor, due regard being had to the juridical relationship between him and the other person; see art. 3:124 BW.

1.6.2. Declaratory judgement

Secondly, the owner and other proprietary title-holders are entitled to request the judge to give a declaratory judgement, either entailing that one's own pretended proprietary right exists (is valid), or that the pretended right or claim of the counterparty does not exist (is invalid). The right to request such a judgement stems from art. 3:302 BW:

> *The judge renders a declaratory judgment on a juridical relationship upon the demand of the person directly concerned.*

This course of action is especially useful when combined with a request for a injunction and a penalty in case of non-compliance (see below).

1.6.3. Tort (injunction, damages)

The owner (and other title-holders) can sue on the basis of tort (art. 6:162 BW) to obtain an *injunction* from the judge, for example forbidding the defendant to disturb the plaintiff in the free and exclusive use of his property. Such an injunction is helpful to the owner in the case of nuisance, hindrance, obstruction, malicious damage to his property, or even when someone else exercises one's authority. The injunction serves to prevent from recurrence of these events and therefore protects against future unlawful acts. It is even possible to obtain an injunction *before* any interference with one's property has actually taken place: the basis of this kind of injunction is that the defendant is legally obliged to

[31] The BW does not use this term, but prefers: "possessor who is not in good faith".
[32] As well as 122 and 123, which have not been dealt with here.

refrain from the tort he is about to commit.[33] Usually, an injunction is combined with the imposition of a penalty in case of non-compiance.

The owner can also sue for **damages**. In principle these damages are awarded in the form of a sum of money, but "the judge may award reparation in a form other than the payment of a sum of money" (art. 6:103 BW): an order to pay damages by way of *restitutio in integrum* or *in natura* is a possibility.

In some cases it is possible for the judge to award damages while refusing to grant an injunction: see art. 6:168 § 1 BW:

> *The judge may reject an Action to obtain an order prohibiting unlawful conduct on the ground that such conduct should be tolerated for reasons of important societal interests. The victim retains his right to reparation of damage according to this title.*

The textbook example is the case in which someone living next to an airport requests an injunction against future nuisance on the basis that the airport violates current noise regulations. The closure of the airport would lead to mass unemployment and severe economic loss, so the injunction ought not to be granted, but the airport's neighbour should not lose his right to receive payment in the form of damages.

1.6.4. Unjustified enrichment

In contrast to the former code (in force between 1838 and 1992) the present code acknowledges the Action arising from unjustified enrichment; art. 6:212. There are four conditions[34]:

- enrichment of the defendant;
- impoverishment of the plaintiff;
- a causal relationship between this enrichment and impoverishment;
- the enrichment has to be unjustified.

When these conditions have been met, the plaintiff is entitled to the payment of damages "to the extent this is reasonable" (art. 6:212 § 1). The extent of the liability has to be assessed as from the moment of the enrichment, not the moment of the summons or the day of the court's judgement.

In recent years, there has been much debate on the legal character of the Action arising from unjustified enrichment. Two extremes can be discerned in this debate;

---

[33] This was also the case before 1992; see HR 18-8-1944, NJ 1944/45, 598. For the current law see *Parl. Gesch.* Boek 6, p. 613, and Asser-Hartkamp, *Verbintenissenrecht. Verbintenis uit de wet* 4-III (Deventer 2002), § 118.

[34] See Bloembergen-Van Dam-Hijma-Valk, *Rechtshandeling en overeenkomst* (3rd ed. Deventer 2001), no. 80.

1. the Action is intended to "fine-tune" the provisions of the code, and therefore its principal function is to supplement.[35]
2. the Action constitutes an exception to the provisions of the code, based on equity: its principal function is to correct wherever equity so demands.[36]

These two approaches are diametrically opposed to one another, but the controversy does not seem to have much practical impact; both sides refer approvingly to the many cases in which the *Hoge Raad* has sustained claims on the basis of unjustified enrichment since 1992.
On one aspect consensus has been reached: the principle of subsidiarity does not apply with regard to the Action arising from unjustified enrichment. This implies that the owner is free to decide whether to litigate on the basis of unjustified enrichment or to commence legal proceedings on another basis (tort, revendication etc.).
In the context of property law, the Action arising from unjustified enrichment is especially important in cases of **accession**, when a thing becomes a "component part" (see art. 3:4 BW) of another thing (the "principal thing; art. 5:14 § 3 BW) belonging to someone else. Even though the implications of accession - loss of ownership on the part of the owner of the component part and simultaneous acquisition by the owner of the principal thing – are based on legal provisions, they are to be considered unjustified. One could say that art. 5:14/20 cause enrichment/impoverishment without justifying them, and therefore they do not preclude an Action arising from unjustified enrichment. There are also provisions which both cause and justify enrichment/impoverishment (for example, the aforementioned art. 3:120 § 1 BW, which assigns natural and civil fruits to the possessor in good faith. See on this subject – which we can leave aside here as it does not relate to transfer – art. 5:14 BW (accession of a movable to a movable) and art. 5:20 (accession of a movable to an immovable).

2. Possession

2.1. Notion of possession; distinction between possessor and detentor

Possession (*bezit*) (together with detention regulated in Book 3 Title 5 BW) is defined in art. 3:107 BW as "the fact of detaining property for oneself". In this definition it is expressed that possession is to be regarded as a species of the genus detention (*houderschap*): possession is the kind of detention which is exercised

[35] See especially W. Snijders, *Ongerechtvaardigde verrijking en het betalingsverkeer.* Studiekring 'Prof.mr. J. Offerhaus' ; nieuwe reeks, no. 7 (Deventer 2001).
[36] See especially A.S. Hartkamp, 'Ongerechtvaardigde verrijking naast overeenkomst en onrechtmatige daad', *WPNR* 6441-6442 (2001).

for oneself. In this respect, detention refers to a factual situation: exercising power over an object. Detention is not defined in the code, but may be inferred form the *travaux préparatoires*. From the fact that detention is not defined it follows that possession lacks a meaningful definition, too. This is no coincidence: the legislator expressed the wish "that the judge, in applying the new provisions on possession, would let himself be guided by the practical function of possession and not by dogmatic considerations."[37]

Next to possession, there is another kind of detention, which is not exercised for oneself, but for someone else. The person who detains an object for someone else is called a detentor (*houder)*. There is some risk of confusion here, as the notion of detentor is reserved for the person detaining for someone else, while the notion of detention has a wider meaning: it can be applied to both the detentor and the possessor.

All property is susceptible to possession and detention: both tangible assets (*zaken*) and rights (*vermogensrechten*). This follows from the definition in art. 3:107 § 1 BW but can also be inferred from the fact that these subjects are regulated in Book 3 BW.

2.1.1. The criterion "detaining property for oneself"

To be in possession implies to have the "animus rem sibi habendi". Nevertheless, the focus of the law is not on the animus itself, but on the behaviour of the possessor, or, to be more precise: on the combination of common opinion and the facts as they appear, with a corrective role for the legal provisions. Compare art. 3:108 BW:

> *Whether somebody detains property and whether he does so for himself or for another, is determined according to common opinion, taking into account the following rules*[38] *and, otherwise, the facts as they appear.*

The legislator has stressed[39] that the words „detaining for himself" are *not* to be read as: "detaining as its title-holder".[40] It provided several arguments for this:

1. the words might suggest that the possessor had to be the title-holder;
2. otherwise, it might be inferred that the possessor had to be *not* the title-holder ("as if he was the title-holder");
3. it could also be maintained that a lessee detains the thing pursuant to the lease contract "as the title-holder".

---

[37] *Parl.Gesch.* Boek 3, p. 424.

[38] This refers to articles 3:109-117 BW.

[39] *Parl. Gesch.* Boek 3, p. 427.

[40] As was mentioned above, the notion of possession applies to all property (corporeal objects and rights), and therefore is placed in Book 3 BW. In this respect, there is an important difference with ownership, which is reserved to things and is placed in Book 5.

The essential question is the following: in what relationship to or under what legal presumption towards others does the person concerned detain the property? Against this background, the use of the criterion „for himself" prevents the aforementioned uncertainties. For example, it can no longer be maintained that a lessee detains "for himself" as he detains pursuant to his relationship with the lessor.[41]

2.1.2. Legal capacity required?

The question whether legal capacity is required to detain for oneself and therefore to be the possessor, receives no attention in the Dutch literature on either possession or legal capacity. The correct answer seems to me that possession in itself does not require legal capacity: Dutch law accepts neither the subjective theory of Von Savigny (focussing on animus) nor the purely objective theory of Von Jhering (focussing on corpus). To determine whether possession occurs one has to look at the circumstances which ordinarily indicate the will to detain for oneself.[42] In doing so, common opinion is decisive (art. 3:108), while the internal will is irrelevant (as has been said above: one has to focus on "the facts as they appear"). This implies that legal capacity is not required for being a possessor.
However, this is irrelevant for the equally important question whether legal capacity is required for *becoming* a possessor. When this involves a legal act, legal capacity is clearly required. Most Dutch authors accept Von Savigny's view that delivery implies a *dingliches Vertrag* (in Dutch: zakelijke overeenkomst), and this can be considered *ius constitutum* (even though there exist a noisy minority of authors which deny the need for a *dingliches Vertrag*). As delivery of movables is effected by the transfer of possession (art. 3:90), the latter has to be considered a legal act, which requires legal capacity on the part of both parties involved. Therefore, a person lacking legal capacity cannot become a possessor of a movable by way of transfer.

2.1.3. Mediate and immediate possession and detention

Like German law, the BW distinguishes between the person who is in actual physical control and the person who exercises control through another person

[41] Important in this context is art. 3:111 BW, which makes it impossible for the detentor like a lessee to change the title of his possession by turning himself into a possessor without informing his counterparty: *A person who has begun detention for another pursuant to a juridical relationship continues to do so under the same title, so long as no change is apparent in his title which results either from an act by the person for whom he holds or from the latter's right having been contested.* This provision is discussed in § 1.2.1, 2.3 and 5.4.2.a.
[42] See A.C. van Schaick, *Rechtsgevolgen en functies van bezit en houderschap*. Mon. NBW A143 (Deventer 2003), p. 12.

physically holding the asset (the detentor). The former is called the immediate possessor, the latter the mediate possessor; see art. 3:107 §§ 2 and 3 BW:

> 2. *A person who possesses property which is not detained for him by another has immediate possession.*
>
> 3. *A person who possesses property which is detained for him by another has mediate possesion.*

The same distinction is made with regard to detention; see art. 3:107 § 4 BW:

> 4. *Mutatis mutandis detention is mediate or immediate.*

It has been pointed out in Dutch legal literature that there are may borderline cases. For example: when one appoints a caretaker to look after one's country house, does that imply that one becomes the immediate possessor? [43] Whatever the answer, the question is not all that important.

2.1.4. Possessor (not) in good faith

Another distinction between different types of possessors is between the possessor in good faith and the possessor not in good faith. The former is (more or less) defined in art. 3:118 § 1 BW:

> *A possessor who believes himself to be the title-holder and is reasonably justified in that belief, is a possessor in good faith.*

Someone who does not meet these requirements is a possessor not in good faith (a separate definition is lacking in the code). In a general context, art. 3:11 BW provides what the requirement of good faith entails:

> *Where good faith of a person is required to produce a juridical effect, such person is not acting in good faith if he knew the facts or the law to which his good faith must relate or if, in the given circumstances, he should know them. Impossibility to inquire does not prevent the person, who had good reasons to be in doubt, from being considered as someone who should know the facts or the law.*

For practical purposes the distinction will not be elaborated upon here; it should be dealt with in the context in which the distinction is relevant (see e.g. above, § 1.4.2, on the revendication under a posssessor in good faith/not in good faith).
Distinctions between different forms of possession based on the intention of the involved persons (the German distinction between *Eigenbesitz* and *Fremdbesitz*) or on the social dependence of the person physically holding the asset from the possessor (the German *Besitzdiener*) have not been adopted in the BW. The

---

[43] See H.C.F. Schoordijk, *Vermogensrecht in het algemeen. Naar Boek 3 van het nieuwe B.W. (titel 1 t/m 5, titel 11)* (Deventer 1986), p. 355.

obvious reason for this is the conviction of the Dutch legislator that the notions 'possession' and 'detention' do not deserve too much attention, while, until 1992, they were given more attention than their practical importance warranted.

2.2. Functions of possession

Dutch doctrine distinguishes between the following functions of possession:[44]

2.2.1. defensive function

This function refers to the protection of possession, which is based on the fact that the person performing acts of possession is usually also the title-holder. This in itself is considered sufficient reason to protect the possessor in his possession; see art. 3:125 BW, which will be dealt with in detail below, § 2.4.

2.2.2. procedural function

The possessor is presumed to be the title-holder (this means that proof of the opposite is accepted). This is enacted in art. 3:119 § 1 BW. The procedural function is related to the aforementioned defensive function, and can even be considered a consequence thereof: both in and outside court the possessor is to be protected on the basis of his possession itself.[45]

2.2.3. acquisitive function

Possession serves as an acquisitive instrument in several ways:

2.2.3.a. occupation

Ownership of a *res nullius* is acquired by taking possession thereof, according to art. 5:4 BW.

---

[44] See Pitlo-Reehuis, *Goederenrecht*, no. 355.

[45] The presumption of art. 3:119 § 1 is set aside in the second paragraph in respect of registered property, where it is established that another party or his predecessor was the title-holder at any time and the possessor could not invoke subsequent acquisition by particular title requiring entry in the registers.

2.2.3.b. prescription

See art. 3:99 § 1 BW:

> *Rights in movable things which are not registered property and rights under documents payable to bearer and order are acquired by a possessor in good faith by uninterrupted possession for three years; other property is acquired by uninterrupted possession for ten years.*

The possessor not in good faith is also entitled to prescription. This follows from art. 3:105 BW:

> *A person, who possesses property at the time of the completion of the prescription of the right of Action to terminate possession, acquires the property even if his possession was not in good faith.*

As revendication is subject to a limitation period of 20 years (art. 3:306 BW), thieves become owners of their loot 20 years after the theft. The wisdom behind the provision of art. 3:105 has been contested by some, who fear that criminals may be induced to steal priceless objects of art, for example Rembrandt's *Night Watch,* in order to hide them for 20 years, after which they are fully entitled to sell them as owners.

2.2.3.c. Transfer

Delivery of the ownership of movables is effected by transfer of possession (art 3:90 § 1 BW). The same applies to rights payable to bearer and order (see art. 3:93 BW). We will deal with this subject in more detail elsewhere.

2.2.3.d. Fruits

Separated natural fruits and civil fruits which have become exigible belong to the possessor in good faith (art. 3:120 § 1 BW). This does not apply to the possessor who is not in good faith: he is obliged to restore to the title-holder the separated natural fruits and the civil fruits which have become exigible (art. 3:121 § 1 BW).

2.2.4. Liability function

For several categories of objects, being its possessor involves liability for any damage the object may cause. This applies to:

- the possessor of a *movable thing* which is known to constitute a special danger for persons or things if it does not meet the standards which, in the given circumstances, may be set for such a thing, unless there would have been no liability if the possessor would have known the danger at the time when it arose (art. 6:173 BW);

- The possessor of a *construction* which does not meet the standards which, in the given circumstances, may be set for it and thereby constitutes a danger for persons or things, unless there would have been no liability if the possessor would have known the danger at the time when it arose. In the case of emphyteusis, the liability rests upon the possessor of the right of emphyteusis. In the case of public roads, it rests upon the public authority in charge of the proper maintenance of the roads; in the case of conduits, it rests upon the person managing them, except to the extent that the conduit is located in a building or work and serves to supply or drain that building or work (art. 6:174 BW);
- The possessor of an *animal*, unless there would have been no liability if the possessor would have had control over the behaviour of the animal which caused the damage (art. 6:179).

Art. 6:181 BW adds to this that where the things, constructions or animals referred to in articles 173, 174, and 179 are used to carry on a business, the liability rests upon the person carrying on this business, unless a construction is involved and the origin of the damage is not related to the carrying on of the business.

2.2.5. Compensation function

Even in cases in which the possessor is obliged to hand over the thing to the owner (e.g. in the case of revendication), the possessor is not left empty-handed: according to art. 3:121 BW, he is entitled to the reimbursement of the costs expended on the property, as well as for damages for which the possessor might be liable toward third persons by reason of his possession; this obligation ceases to the extent that the possessor has been indemnified by the fruits of the property and the other benefits which he has drawn from it. The judge may reduce the reimbursement due if full reimbursement would result in an inequitable advantage for the possessor over the title-holder. The possessor not in good faith is entitled to reimbursement of the costs which he has expended on the property or which he has made to produce the fruits only to the extent that his claim can be based on the rules regarding unjust enrichment; art. 3:121 BW. See above, § 1.4.2 and 1.6.1.

2.3. Acquisition of possession

In art. 3:112 BW, three forms of acquisition of possession are distinguished: by taking possession, by transfer of possession and by succession by general title.

2.3.1. Taking possession (occupatio)

A person takes possession of property by acquiring actual control of it (art. 3:113 § 1 BW). Taking possession is possible with regard to both things and patrimonial rights.
The control of the property should be exercised in such a manner that it is made manifest that the former possessor is no longer in that position; common opinion has to be the guideline here. If the property is in the possession of another, isolated acts of control are insufficient for taking possession (Art. 3:113 § 2 BW).
The acts which could indicate taking possession of immovable property are usually performed periodically (non-permanently). Nevertheless, it is necessary that these acts vis-à-vis the property are performed with (according to common opinion) a degree of permanency (stability).[46]

2.3.2. Transfer of possession

Possession can be transferred either corporeal or by a bilateral declaration without material acts; the former is provided for in art. 3:114, the latter in art. 3:115 BW.

2.3.2.a. Corporeal transfer of possession

Art. 3:114 BW provides:

> *A possessor transfers his possession by enabling the acquirer to exercise such control over the property as he himself was able to exercise over it.*

The most obvious way of providing possession in this manner is by handing over the object (*traditio vera*) or any other act which gives direct possession over the object, such as the handing over of keys (*traditio symbolica).*
Transfer of possession can only be performed by someone who is the possessor himself. A detentor cannot transfer possession simply because he does not have possession himself. Nevertheless, the BW acknowledges that a detentor can *give* possession, notwithstanding the fact that he lacks possession himself. See art. 3:90, which states that the delivery of a movable thing is made by giving possession to the acquirer; in this manner it is indicated that the delivery may be performed by both a possessor and a detentor.

---

[46] *Asser-Mijnssen-De Haan* 3-I, no. 186.

2.3.2.b. Transfer of possession by bilateral declaration

Art. 3:115 BW (traditio ficta)[47] acknowledges three forms of transfer of possession, effected by mere agreement (bilateral declaration, constituting a legal act):

- **Traditio constitutum possessorium (art. 3:115 under a):** the alienator possesses the thing and henceforth detains it for the acquirer by virtue of a stipulation made at the time of delivery. Traditio constitutum possessorium cannot be performed by a detentor: this follows both from the opening words of art. 3:115 (the article deals with *transer* of possession, but see below) and from art. 3:111 (*A person who has begun detention for another pursuant to a juridical relationship continues to do so under the same title, so long as no change is apparent in his title which results either from an act by the person for whom he holds or from the latter's right having been contested*). The scope of traditio constitutu possessorium is diminished even further by art. 3:90 § 2: *Delivery of a thing which remains in the hands of the alienator has no effect with respect to a third person who has a prior right to the thing, until the time when the thing has come into the hands of the acquirer, unless the third person has consented to the alienation.* The effect of articles 3:90 § 2 and 3:11 combined is that consitutum possessorium is considered a "lesser form" of traditio (which is explained and justified by the lack of publicity of consitutum possessorium).
- **traditio brevi manu (art. 3:115 under b):** the acquirer was the detentor of the thing for the alienator. This form of transfer may also be exercised by a detentor.[48]
- **Tradition longa manu (art. 3:115 under c):** a third party detained the thing for the alienator and detains it for the recipient after the transfer. In this event possession does not pass until the third party has acknowledged the transfer or has been notified thereof by the alienator or acquirer. Traditio longa manu by a detentor has been acknowledged by the *Hoge Raad*.[49]

---

[47] See L.P.W. van Vliet, *Transfer of movables in German, French, English and Dutch law* (Nijmegen 2000), *passim*.

[48] It is common opinion that traditio brevi manu may also be performed by a detentor (in which case the provision is to be applied analogously). In that case, possession is not *transferred*, but *given*. The first words of art. 3:115 suggest (apparently incorrectly for traditio brevi manu and, as we will see below, longa manu) that traditio by bilateral agreement can only be performed by a possessor.

[49] HR 1-5-1987, NJ 1988, 852. See also HR 18-9-1987, NJ 1988, 983.

Not included in the BW, but acknowledged by the *Hoge Raad*, is the *traditio sine manu.*[50] This term is used to indicate the traditio (a mixture between constitutum possessorium and brevi manu) between two people who before and after the transfer exercise shared control over the transferred object. This is the case when a thing is transferred between husband and wife, for example.
See on transfer of possession in more detail below, § 5.4 (and in particular § 5.4.2).

2.3.3. Succession by general title

Art. 3:116 BW provides that the possession and detention of the successor by general title is of the same quality and subject to the same defects as that of his predecessor. Succession by general title occurs through inheritance, fusion of patrimonies (in case of marriage) and through succession to the patrimony of a legal person which has ceased to exist (art. 3:80 § 2).
The purpose of art. 3:116 is to establish that the nature and quality of the possession and detention are not influenced by the fact that they change hands in the case of inheritance, fusion of patrimonies or succession to the patrimony of a legal person; when the predecessor was not in good faith, the successor is neither, even if, in reality, he was in good faith.
The importance of this provision manifests itself in particular in the case of prescription: *A person who succeeds to the possession of another by general title continues an already running prescription* (art. 3:102 § 1). This means that even the successor not in good faith continues the already running prescription, as long as the predecessor was in good faith. This differs from prescription in case of acquisition of possession otherwise than by general title: in that case the successor has to be in good faith himself (see art. 3:102 § 2).

2.4. Protection of possession

The BW awards the possessor real protection in art. 3:125 (more or less after the example of the ancient Actio *Publiciana*), which reads as follows:

> 1. *He who has acquired possession of property can, on the basis of a subsequent loss of or disturbance in the possession, institute the same Actions against third persons to recover the property and to remove the disturbance as the title-holder of the property. Nevertheless, these Actions must be instituted within the year following the loss or disturbance.*

[50] See HR 18-2-1966, NJ 1967, 109 (*Goubitz/Klinger*) and HR 7-3-1975, NJ 1976, 190 (*Lutgens/Karsmakers*).

2. *The Action is rejected if the defendant has a better right than the plaintiff to the detention of the property or if he has performed the disturbing acts pursuant to a better right, unless the defendant has taken possession from the plaintiff or has disturbed his possession in a violent or surreptitious manner.*
3. *Nothing in this article deprives the possessor, even after the expiry of the year referred to in the first paragraph, or the detentor of the possibility, should there be grounds, to institute an Action on the basis of an unlawful act.*

The purpose of the provision is to give protection to the possessor against those who have a lesser right to the property. Protection is given to any possessor; whether or not he is in good faith is irrelevant.

The possessor can (within a year following the loss or disturbance) institute the same Actions as the title-holder (see § 1). In the first place, this refers to the revendication (art. 5:2 BW), which is especially valuable when the defendant has been declared bankrupt. Other Actions to terminate an unlawful situation qualify also (for example, the denial of a pretended dismembered right[51]), as well as accessory Actions like requesting an injunction under forfeit of a penalty.

The second paragraph states that the possessor cannot institute the Action against a defendant who has a better right to the property. This refers in the first place to the title-holder, but applies also to the detentor (for example, the renter who is entitled to continued use of the property) and to the (former) possessor of the property who was the victim of theft.

Recently the *Hoge Raad* has applied this provision analogously to the right of retention.[52] The retentor who loses control of the thing (and thereby loses his right of retention) is entitled to reclaim it under the same conditions as an owner, according to art. 3:295 BW. If successful, the right of retention is revived. Now the *Hoge Raad* has ruled that the (former) retentor is not entitled to reclaim the thing when it has come into the control of the owner. Justification for this decision was found in the analogous rule of art. 3:125 § 2 BW.

There is an important exception to the rule that the possessor is not entitled to reclaim the property against someone with a better right: to prevent him from taking the law into his own hands, the Action is allowed against someone who has acted unlawfully („in a violent or surreptitious manner"). This implies that the owner should not 'steal' his own property from a possessor who is unwilling to hand it to him voluntarily: in reaction, the possessor would be entitled to institute

[51] See Hartkamp, *Compendium*, no. 119.

[52] HR 20-9-2002, NJ 2004, 171 (*Van der Wal/Duinstra*).

an action to recover it, even if that would re-establish the deadlock between owner and possessor.[53]

The importance of the third paragraph of art. 3:125 lies in the fact that it stresses that the possessor who is the victim of interference, hindrance, theft etc. is not obliged to use the Actions of art. 3:125 § 1 BW: he can opt for an Action based on tort. This applies not only to the situation in which the period of one year, mentioned in art. 3:125 § 1, has passed, but also before that.[54] Obviously, this course is not to be preferred above the real Action of art. 3:125 against someone who is bankrupt. In summary proceedings, on the other hand, the tort-based Action has the advantage of a speedy outcome.[55]

3. Personal right and proprietary protection

3.1. Introduction

This section deals with the question whether the various rights to hold or to acquire a movable are always obligatory rights or can also be or equal rights in rem. The starting point should be that Dutch patrimonial law has, as said above in § 1.2, from HR 3-3-1905, W. 1905, no. 8191 onwards maintained a fairly sharp distinction between rights in rem and rights in personam. The distinction has lost some of its sharpness in recent decades, but the disctinction also characterizes the new BW of 1992. Justification for this is found in the importance which is attached in Dutch property law (old and new) to the principle of publicity: '*drittwirkung*' of rights requires (and presupposes) that the acquisition and existence of that right is knowable.

3.2. A proprietary position for the financial lessee or the buyer in case of eservation of title?

Against this background it is understandable that common opinion is not prepared to award a right in rem to the (financial) lessee. Not all authors share this view, however: in his thesis on leasing, J.J. van Hees argued in 1997 that the position of the lessee has to be qualified as a proprietary claim on the object of the financial

---

[53] In the just mentioned case (HR 20-9-2002, NJ 2004, 171, in which the *Hoge Raad* decided that the action of the retentor under art. 3:295 BW cannot be used against the owner) the Procurator General proposed to accept an exception similar to that mentioned in art. 3:125 § 2 for the situation in which the owner had acted unlawfully against the possessor. The *Hoge Raad*, however, did not comment on this suggestion (as it was not relevant to the case at hand).

[54] See Pitlo-Reehuis, *Goederenrecht*, no. 401 ff.

[55] See W. Schenk and J.H. Blaauw, *Het kort geding, B. bijzonder deel* (Deventer 1995), pp. 91 ff.

lease:[56] both the lessor and the lessee should in this view be regarded as owners. Van Hees maintains that his view is supported by other kinds of "relative ownership" in Dutch law: in case of seizure (art. 453a *Wetboek van Burgerlijke Rechtsvordering* = Code of Civil Procedure), the Actio Pauliana (art. 3:45 BW and art. 42 *Faillissementswet* = Bankruptcy Act) and constitutum possessorium (art. 3:90 § 2): in all these instances, the acquirer of an object is to be regarded as its owner, *except* against certain stakeholders (creditors, third persons with a prior right etc.). By others[57] it has been pointed out, however, that in all these cases of "relative ownership", there is always only one owner in each relationship: so the acquirer in case of transfer constitutum possessorium is considered to be the owner with regard to third persons, but with regard to persons with a prior right he is not. In this view it is impossible that both lessor and lessee are considered to be owners simultaneously.
Just as most Dutch legal scholars are not prepared to award the financial lessee a proprietary position, they refuse to regard the acquirer in case of transfer under suspensive condition (see art. 3:91) as more than a mere detentor. In case of reservation of title (art. 3:92 BW) ownership is not transferred until the buyer performs his obligation: before that, the buyer has no right in rem on his purchase.

3.3. 'Vormerkung' with regard to registered property

An important exception to the rule that in the case of transfer, ownership changes hands at the moment of delivery and not before, has recently (September 1, 2003) been introduced in the BW with regard to registered property (especially houses) which should be mentioned here even though movables are our main concern. In case of a sale of registered property, the sale can be entered in the public register: this entry safeguards the buyer against events like transfer, seizure or lease of the property, or it being put under administration, and even the bankruptcy of the seller. However, the entry of the sale should within six months be followed by the delivery of the property (thereby finalizing the transfer of ownership); otherwise the protection of the entry in the public registers loses force with retroactive effect. See art. 7: 3 §§ 1-4 BW.
With regard to other property no changes have been introduced. Therefore, there is no proprietary effect connected to options to buy, to sale on approval, to the agreement to conclude a contract later on (*Vorvertrag*) or the right to repurchase.[58]

---

[56] J.J. van Hees, *Leasing*. Serie Onderneming en Recht 8 (Zwolle 1997), pp. 108-111 and *passim*.
[57] See especially J.E. Fesevur in his review of Van Hees' thesis in *RM Themis* 2000/4, p.144-148. See also the review of the same thesis by A.F. Salomons in *Weekblad voor Privaatrecht, Notariaat en Registratie* 2000/6414, p. 598-602.
[58] I leave aside the provisions on repurchase agreements which have been introduced by the implementation of the Collateral Directive of June 6, 2002 (2002/47/EG) (see art. 7:51-56 BW).

3.4. Indirect representation

Finally, proprietary protection is given to the principal in case of acquisition through an agent; see art. 3:110 BW:

> *Where there exists a juridical relationship between two persons to the effect that what one of them will acquire in a specified manner will be detained by him for the other, the former detains for the latter what has been acquired by him in the performance of the juridical relationship.*

This provision, the enactment of which in 1992 ended a long debate, implies the enactment of the so-called "direct doctrine" or "doctrine of direct acquisition". It means that the principal automatically becomes the possessor of the property which his agent acquires for him. With regard to movables, this has the effect that the principal acquires ownership, as the delivery of movables is effected by the transfer of possession (art. 3:90 § 1). In 1996, the *Hoge Raad* stated that the direct doctrine, the validity of which the *Hoge Raad* explicitly founded on art. 3:110 BW, is only applicable to goods which are delivered through the transfer of possession.[59] This is not to say, however, that art. 3:110 itself is reserved for goods which are delivered in that way.

We can conclude that for the application of art. 3:110 there are (no more than) two requirements:

- the judicial relationship between the two persons should have the effect that what one of them will acquire will be detained by him for the other;
- the acquisition has to take place in the performance of that juridical relationship.

The scope of art. 3:110 is furthermore not at all restricted to agency: it also covers acquisitions on behalf of another in cases of lease (by the lessee), loan (by the borrower), encumbered right (e.g. by the pledge-holder) etc. The juridical relationship underlying the acquisition does not have to be created by contract: management of the affairs of another, for example, may create a similar juridical relationship. Another example: the detentor of a thing creates out of that a new thing under orders of the owner of the original thing: that owner acquirers ownership of the new thing pursuant to art. 5:16 BW, whereas art. 3:110 attributes to him the possession of the new thing.[60] See on this subject also below, Section 7.

---

[59] HR 23-9-1994, NJ 1996, 461 (*Kas-Associatie/Drying*).

[60] Hartkamp, *Compendium*, no. 111. See for other examples *Losbladige vermogensrecht*, annotation 8 on art. 3:110 (J.D.A. den Tonkelaar).

4. Field of application and definitions

4.1. Field of application

Transfer of property in general is dealt with in art. 3:84 BW: this provision (which says that a transfer requires delivery pursuant to a valid title by the person who has the right to dispose of the property) applies to all goods (that is: both things and patrimonial rights, art. 3:1 BW). In articles 3:89-97 (with the exception of art. 3:92 and 3:92a) the various forms of delivery are enumerated; see the following scheme:

Article	Object of delivery	Form of delivery
Art. 3:89	Immovable things and other registered property	Notarial deed intended for that purpose and drawn up between the parties, followed by its entry in the public registers provided for that purpose. Either the acquirer or the alienator may have the deed registered.
Art. 3:90	Movable things which are unregistered property and which are under the control of the alienator	Giving possession of the thing to the acquirer
Art. 3:91	Things referred to in the preceding article delivered in the performance of an obligation to transfer under suspensive condition	Giving the acquirer control over the thing.
Art. 3:93	Right payable to bearer, the instrument of which is under the control of the alienator	Delivery of the document in the manner and with the effects as specified in articles 90, 91, and 92.
	Right payable to order which is under the control of the alienator	The same, provided that the document is also endorsed
Art. 3:94	Other rights to be exercised against one or more specifically determined persons	Either by a deed intended for that purpose and notice thereof given by the alienator or acquirer to those persons or by an authentic deed or a registered deed under private writing without notification thereof to those persons

Art. 3:95	In cases other than those provided for in articles 89 - 94	A deed intended for that purpose.
Art. 3:96	Delivery of a share in property	Delivery is made analogously to the delivery of that property and has analogous effects
Art. 3:97	Future property	(Delivery is made analogously to the delivery of that property)

Art. 3:90 applies to movable things which are unregistered property and which are under the control of the alienator. Movable registered property (certain categories of aircraft and ships) is delivered in the manner specified in art. 3:89 BW (notarial deed and entry in public registers, see above). Movable things which are not under the control of the alienator (especially stolen things, e.g. to an insurance company) are delivered in the manner specified in art. 3:95: a deed intended for that purpose. One category of goods which is not dealt with in Book 3 BW is the registered (inscribed) share. Such a share in a corporation is delivered by a deed, executed by a notary practising in the Netherlands, intended for that purpose and drawn up between the parties (art. 2:86 § 1 BW). The same applies to a registered share in a private company with limited liability (art. 2:196 § 1 BW). The articles mentioned specifically list the prescribed contents of the notarial deed (the title of transfer, number and kind of shares involved, information on the legal form and location of the legal persons involved, etc.).

Intellectual property rights are not included in the *Burgerlijk Wetboek* but dealt with in separate laws. These laws specify the manner in which these rights are delivered (art. 3:84 on transfer in general is applicable). Art. 2 § 2 *Auteurswet* (Copyright Law) provides that a copyright is delivered by a deed intended for that purpose. A patent recht is delivered by a bilateral deed which may be entered in the Patent Registry of the Patent Board, art. 65 Rijksoctrooiwet (Patent Law). Transfer of a trademark is possible, provided that it is established in written form (see art. 11 *Beneluxwet op de merken,* Benelux Trade Mark Act, art. 13 *Beneluxwet inzake tekeningen en modellen,* Benelux Drawings and Designs Act). Finally, plant breeders' rights are delivered by a deed (art. 48 *Zaaizaad en Plantgoedwet,* Seeds and Planting Materials Act). Entry of trademarks and plant breeders' rights in public registers is possible and advisable as it has effect against third persons.

4.2. Definitions

Art. 3:3 gives a definition of movable and immovable:

1. *Immovable are land, unextracted minerals, plants attached to land buildings and works durably united with land, either directly or through incorporation with other buildings or works.*
2. *All things which are not immovable, are movable.*

Even though the article does not state this *expressis verbis,* the distinction between movable and immovable only applies to things (corporeal objects), not to patrimonial rights.

The distinction between tangible ("lichamelijke") and intangible ("onlichamelijke") property which was made in the previous civil code, is not maintained in the code of 1992. Obviously, things (art. 3:2) are tangible and patrimonial rights (art. 3:6) are intangible.

There is not much debate on the status of money in property law, even though this is far from clear and the subject is an important one. Coins are certainly to be considered movable things, and therefore they are delivered by giving the possession of them by the alienator to the acquirer. The status of bank notes is more difficult: on the one hand, they can be considered as rights to be exercised against the European Central Bank, but, on the other, this does not explain why no claim against the ECB remains when the bank notes are lost (e.g. through fire). Another problem of the notion of ownership with regard to bank notes is the fact that the bearer usually does not specify them, whilst specification is required for ownership.[61] The suggestion has been made by Houtappel – so far, without success - to add a second paragraph to art. 3:1 BW, stating that property that serves as general tender, is money.[62]

No less complex is the status of electricity, due to its dualistic nature. The Dutch Supreme Court has ruled in a criminal case that electricity is susceptible to theft.[63] Several authors have warned, however, that this does not imply that in private law electricity has to be acqnowledged as a corporeal object (a thing) and as susceptible to ownership, as is the case in Swiss and Italian law and reportedly also in Austrian and French law. Consensus has not yet been achieved, even though most authors agree that the issue is not an important one.[64]

---

[61] See Snijders/Rank-Berenschot, *Goederenrecht,* no. 33.

[62] J.C. Houtappel, *Geld of vordering in het Nederlands privaatrecht* (thesis Amsterdam 1996), p. 95.

[63] HR 23-3-1921, NJ 1921, 564, W. 10728.

[64] See *Asser-Mijnssen-De Haan* 3-I, § 57. See also M.B.M. Loos, *De energieleveringsovereenkomst. Algemene voorwaarden voor de levering van energie aan consumenten* (Tilburg 1998), pp. 51-59. Loos himself advocates the view that electricity is a thing and therefore susceptible to ownership.

The status of gas does not provide similar difficulties. Gas is to be considered a thing, as long as it is put in a tank, a bottle or a similar device (because only corporeal objects which are susceptible to human control are things: art. 3:2 BW).

Part II: Derivative acquisition

5. Which system of transfer is used?

5.1. Basic characteristics / overview

5.1.1. Unititular concept of the transfer of ownership

Dutch property law adheres to the principle of unititular (uniform) ownership transfer. This means that all rights and powers connected with ownership – such as the right to dispose of the property, the right to revendicate (provided the property is a thing), the protection against the insolvency of the transferor (separatism), the right to enjoy the fruits of the property etc. – pass to the acquirer at one moment in time. Therefore, fragmentation of ownership in the sense that the transferor is the owner for some purposes while the transferee is the owner for others, is excluded: simultaneous ownership by different persons with regard to one object (other than joint ownership thereof) would be detrimental to legal certainty.
However, the notion of *relative ownership* is not alien to Dutch property law. For example: annulment of a transfer by a creditor of the transferor on the basis of the Actio *pauliana*[65] has the effect that the transfer has no effect with regard to the creditor but is nonetheless valid as far as everyone else is concerned. It is customary to label the acquirer the relative owner: to the creditor, the alienator is still owner, but to the rest of the world, the acquirer is. A similar phenomenon is to be seen in the law of seizure and in the effects of *traditio constitutum possessorium* (application of art. 3:90 § 2, discussed elsewhere).

5.1.2. The same transfer rules applicable to all kinds of obligations

The general provision on transfer of property (art. 3:84 § 1 BW) determines that the transfer of property requires delivery pursuant to a valid title by the person who has the right to dispose of the property. All kinds of legal acts can function as 'valid title': the obligation to transfer ownership from a salcs contract or a donation (which in Dutch law is also a contract), an obligation to pay damages or to correct unjustified enrichment, an obligation to pay or give something under a

[65] See art. 3:45 BW: *If a debtor, in the performance of a juridical act to which he is not obligated, knew or ought to have known that his act would adversely affect the recourses of one or several of his creditors against his patrimony, the act may be annulled; any creditor whose recourses have been adversely affected by the juridical act may invoke this ground for annulment, irrespective of whether his claim has arisen before or after the act.* See on this article below, § 8.2.

court order, etc. The notion 'title' is commonly understood to mean: a legal relationship (or legal ground, legal fact) that underlies a transfer *and* serves as justification for that transfer.[66]

5.1.3. Basic transfer requirements

Firstly, the asset involved should be transferable. Art. 3:83 § 1 BW provides that "ownership, dismembered rights and debts are transferable, unless this is precluded by law or by the nature of the right". This means that all assets are in principle transferable and that this transferability cannot be excluded by agreement.[67] The underlying thought is that the free movement of assets should not be restricted.[68]

As said above, art. 3:84 § 1 BW provides that the transfer of property requires delivery pursuant to a valid title by the person who has the right to dispose of the property. In sum, Dutch law requires for a valid transfer: (1) a valid title, (2) the right to dispose thereof and (3) delivery. Those are constitutive requirements, meaning that the transfer is not valid if one of those requirements is not met, unless a provision for the protection of third parties could successfully be invoked.[69]

5.1.3.a. Valid title

See § 5.1.2: 'title' is the legal relationship which underlies and justifies the transfer. The kind of obligations on which a transfer of ownership can be based and the consequences of a defective title on the transfer of ownership will be dealt with in § 5.3.1. respectively § 5.3.2.

5.1.3.b. Right to dispose

'To dispose' is to perform an act with respect to an asset, by which the asset is alienated (transferred to a new owner) or is encumbered with a dismembered right.[70] The right to dispose may stem from ownership, a legal act or the law.[71]

---

66 This definition was introduced in 1974 by A.S. Hartkamp, the current procurator general (*Procureur-Generaal)* at the *Hoge Raad* in his article "Het begrip leveringstitel", *WPNR* 5267/5268. See *Asser-Mijnssen-De Haan* 3-I, p. 209; Pitlo-Reehuis, *Goederenrecht*, p. 82. See below,
Section 7.

67 The law makes an exception for debts. The second paragraph of art. 3:83 BW provides: '*Transferability of debts can also be excluded by agreement between creditor and debtor.*'.

68 *Parl. Gesch.* Boek 3, p. 314; *Asser-Mijnssen-De Haan* 3-I, pp. 159-160.

69 Pitlo-Reehuis, *Goederenrecht*, p. 81.

70 Pitlo-Reehuis, *Goederenrecht*, pp. 110-111.

71 Van Vliet, *Transfer of movables*, p. 155.

The principal rule is that the owner is entitled to dispose. This right to dispose belongs in principle exclusively to the owner.[72] However, the owner may give permission to another person to dispose of his asset. An example is indirect agency. If the owner orders an undisclosed commercial agent to sell and transfer an asset, the legal act of sale and transfer will be made in the agent's name. By ordering the transaction the owner gives the agent the right to dispose of the asset. Another example is the sale and transfer of goods under a retention of title clause. If there is a practical need for the buyer to resell the goods before full payment of the price, the seller, who is still the owner, may allow the buyer to sell and transfer his goods. The seller's permission gives the buyer a right to dispose of the seller's goods.[73]
Furthermore, the right to dispose could be based on the law. An example is art. 68 *Bankruptcy Act*. This article provides that the trustee in bankruptcy (*faillissementscurator*) is entitled to dispose of the insolvent's assets.[74] Another example is to be found in art. 3:248 BW, which gives the pledgee the right to dispose of another's assets, provided that all requirements for execution are fulfilled.[75]
As a valid transfer needs to be performed by someone who has the right to dispose, pursuant to art. 3:84 BW, a transfer by someone who is not privileged to dispose is void. Nevertheless, such transfer could be valid if the acquirer of the property could successfully invoke one of the provisions for the protection of third parties: art. 3:24-26, 36, 86 and 88 BW.
Art. 3:86 BW protects the acquirer in good faith against a lack of privilege to dispose of the transferor of – among other things – movables, which were in the power of the transferor. Art. 3:86 § 1 BW provides:

> *Although an alienator lacks the right to dispose of the property, a transfer pursuant to articles 90, 91 or 93 of a movable thing, unregistered property, or a right payable to bearer or order is valid, if the transfer is not by gratuitous title and if the acquirer is in good faith.*

But the law makes an exception in the case of theft. The third paragraph of art. 3:86 BW provides:

> *Nevertheless, the owner of a movable thing, who has lost its possession through theft, may revendicate it during a period of three years from the day of theft, unless*

[72] Pitlo-Reehuis, *Goederenrecht*, pp. 111-112.
[73] Van Vliet, *Transfer of movables*, pp. 155-156.
[74] Art. 23 Bankruptcy Act provides that the debtor loses the privilege to dispose of his assets when he is declared insolvent.
[75] Van Vliet, *Transfer of movables*, p. 155.

(a) *the thing has been acquired by a natural person, not acting in the exercise of a profession or business, from an alienator whose business it is to deal with the public in similar things, otherwise than at a public sale, on business premises destined for that purpose, being an immovable structure or part thereof with the land belonging thereto, and provided that the alienator be in the ordinary exercise of his business, or*

(b) *money or documents payable to bearer or order are involved.*

A further condition for the protection of art. 3:86 is to be found in art. 3:87 § 1 BW:

> *An acquirer, who is asked within three years from his acquisition to identify the alienator, must, without delay, provide all information which is necessary to trace that person or which he could have considered as being sufficient for that purpose at the time of his acquisition. If he does not comply with this obligation, he may not invoke the protection which articles 86 and 86a afford to an acquirer in good faith.*

This so-called *wegwijsplicht* (duty to show the way) does not apply to money (art. 3:87 § 2 BW).

Art. 3:88 § 1 BW is the twin of art. 3:86 for registered property and claims, and according to some authors is also applicable to movables which were not in the power of the transferor at the time of the transfer and therefore have been transferred by deed pursuant to art. 3:95. Its scope is more limited, however, because of the extra conditions for its application (but note that neither the condition of transfer for value and the 'duty to show the way' apply in the context of art. 3:88) Art. 3:88 § 1 provides:

> *Although an alienator lacks the right to dispose of property, the transfer of registered property, a nominative right or other property to which article 86 does not apply, is valid if the acquirer is in good faith and if the lack of the right to dispose results from the invalidity of a previous transfer, which itself did not result from the lack of the right to dispose of the alienator at the time.*

Articles 3:24, 25 and 26 BW protect the acquirer of registered objects in good faith against the incompleteness or incorrectness of public registers. Art. 3:24 § 1 BW provides that 'if, at the time of registration of a juridical act to acquire a right to registered property by particular title, a fact which is also susceptible of entry in the registers was not entered in reference to that registered property, this fact cannot be opposed to the acquirer, unless he knew it'. However, this does not apply to '(a) facts which according to their nature are susceptible of entry in a register of civil status, a matrimonial property register or a successions register, even if the fact cannot be registered in a given instance because the law of the Netherlands does not apply to it, (b) placement under and termination of curatorship, entered in the register of curatorship, (c) judgments entered in the bankruptcy register or in the register of receivership, (d) acceptance and rejection of a succession, (e) prescription' (art. 3:24 § 2 BW). Neither does the first paragraph of art. 3:24 BW apply to 'successions and testamentary dispositions which were not registered at the moment of the registration of the juridical act, but which were thereafter entered in the registers within three months of the death of the deceased (whether a testator or not) (art. 3:24 § 3 BW).

Art. 3:25 BW provides that 'if, at the time of registration of a juridical act to acquire a right to registered property by particular title, a fact pertaining to that registered property was entered in the registers pursuant to an authentic deed in which this fact was authenticated by a civil servant, the inaccuracy of this fact cannot be invoked against the acquirer, unless he knew it or could have known of the possibility thereof by consulting the registers'. In addition, art. 3:26 BW provides that 'if, at the time of registration of a juridical act to acquire a right to registered property by particular title, an inaccurate fact pertaining to that registered property was entered in the registers, the inaccuracy of this fact cannot be invoked against the acquirer by a person who could reasonably have ensured the conformity of the registers with the reality, unless the acquirer knew the inaccuracy or could have known of the possibility thereof by consulting the registers'.

Art. 3:36 BW, the most indefinite provision on third party protection in the BW, protects a third party, who acted in good faith based on the existence of a legal relation alleged by another, which in fact never came into existence, or meanwhile has been changed or annulled. The legal act, which the third party performed as a result of the alleged legal relation, could not be opposed to this party. Art. 3:36 BW provides that 'a third person who under the circumstances reasonably bases an assumption as to the creation, existence or extinction of a juridical relationship on a declaration or conduct of another, and has acted reasonably on the basis of the accuracy of that assumption, cannot have invoked against him the inaccuracy of that assumption by the other person'. If, for example, A and B draw up a deed for tax purposes which states that A owes € 100 to B, whereas in reality he owes only € 50, and B persuades C to buy his claim against A, showing C the deed, C will be under the false impression that he receives a claim worth € 100. As A, by drawing up the deed, is to blame for the incorrect assumption of C with regard to the true value of the claim, he is not entitled to rely on that against him: A will have to pay € 100 to C (but of course he may claim payment of compensation by B).

5.1.3.c. Delivery

Delivery (*levering*) is the legal act by which the obligation to transfer (the title) is actually carried out. The delivery brings about the transfer of the property involved if all other conditions of a valid transfer are met. In short, delivery is the legal act, transfer is the legal consequence.[76] The concept of delivery is regarded as consisting of two elements: (1) an agreement in which the transferor and the transferee express their common intention to transfer the asset involved (the transferor declares that he will transfer ownership of the asset and the acquirer declares that he will accept ownership thereof) and (2) an act by which the transferor and the transferee manifest their common intention to transfer.[77] The first element could be qualified as a real agreement (*goederenrechtelijke overeenkomst*)[78] and is elaborated in § 5.7. For the second element see § 5.4.2.

5.2. Categorization of transfer system

5.2.1. Causal or abstract?

Under the old civil code of 1838 it was disputed whether the Dutch transfer system was abstract or causal.[79] Not until 1950 did the *Hoge Raad* decide the question explicitly in favour of the causal system.[80] The new 1992 civil code codified this choice in art. 3:84 § 1 BW by unequivocally requiring that a transfer should be based on a valid title.[81] Accordingly, delivery without a valid title (e.g. after annulment) does not bring about a transfer of the asset involved.

5.2.2. Consensual or tradition system?

The entering into a sales contract, which obliges the seller to transfer an asset to the buyer, does not bring about the transfer of the asset, as would be the case under French law. The parties need to perform a further legal act in order to finalize the transfer. The obligation to transfer needs to be carried out by means of the actual delivery of the asset. Upon delivery the acquirer is acknowledged as the (new) owner of the asset.[82] Thus, Dutch law has a tradition system.[83]

---

[76] *Parl. Gesch.* Boek 3, p. 308; *Asser-Mijnssen-De Haan* 3-I, p. 164; Pitlo-Reehuis, *Goederenrecht*, p. 69.
[77] *Asser-Mijnssen-De Haan* 3-I, p. 162 and 164.
[78] *Asser-Mijnssen-De Haan* 3-I, p. 164.
[79] *Asser-Mijnssen-De Haan* 3-I, p. 207-209.
[80] HR 5-5-1950, NJ 1951, 1 (*Damhof/Staat*)
[81] *Asser-Mijnssen-De Haan* 3-I, p. 207-209; Van Vliet, *Transfer of movables*, p. 196-199.
[82] Pitlo-Reehuis, *Goederenrecht*, p. 81.
[83] Van Vliet, *Transfer of movables*, p. 133.

5.2.3. Requirement of payment?

Dutch law does not recognize a requirement of payment for the acquisition by a transfer based upon a sales contract. A sales contract brings about two obligations: one for the seller to transfer (the ownership of) the asset concerned[84] and another for the buyer to pay the price agreed upon.[85] Those are separate, although not completely independent, obligations. The seller transfers the asset to the buyer based upon an existing obligation to transfer, which is a valid title for transfer. Thus, the buyer acquires the asset, even if he has not yet fulfilled his obligation to pay. If the buyer does not pay, the seller could terminate the sales contract (see for the consequences of termination § 5.3.2.).
However, termination gives the seller only a personal claim against the buyer to return (by transfer) the asset involved. But the law provides some other ways in which the seller could procure that the ownership returns to him by operation of law in case of non-payment, or that the ownership is not transferred to the buyer until he actually pays. Firstly, the seller could exercise his right of revendication (see § 5.3.2). Furthermore, the seller could enter into the contract on the resolutive condition of non-payment of the agreed price (see § 5.3.2) or under a reservation of title clause. Art. 3:92 § 1 BW provides:

> *Where a contract is intended to reserve to one party the ownership of a thing which is placed under the control of the other party, until a performance owed by the latter has been made, the former is presumed to obligate himself to the transfer of the thing to the latter under a suspensive condition of that performance.*

Obviously, the transferor is entitled to suspend the execution of his obligation to deliver in case the transferee does not pay the price, assuming that the transferee was obliged to perform before the transferor or both of them had to perform simultaneously and the transferor has good reason to fear that the transferee will not in fact pay. This follows from art. 6:262-263 BW (the enactment of the so-called exceptio non adimpleti contractus).

5.3. Valid obligation

5.3.1. Obligations on which the transfer of ownership can be based

Beforehand, a short outline of the place of acquisition through transfer in the system of acquisition in general may be helpful.

---

[84] Art. 7:9 § 1 BW provides: *The seller is obliged to transfer the ownership of the thing sold and to deliver it with its accessories. (...).*
[85] Art. 7:26 BW provides: *The buyer is obliged to pay the price.*

Art. 3:80 § 1 BW provides that 'property is acquired by general and by particular title'. Acquisition by general title is acquisition by which a whole patrimony, or a proportional part thereof, passes to another.[86] 'Property is acquired by general title through inheritance[87], fusion of patrimonies[88] or succession to the patrimony of a legal person, which has ceased to exist[89]' (art. 3:80 § 2 BW). In the case of acquisition by general title the acquirer continues the position of the alienator, i.e., the acquirer is bound by the personal rights and obligations which previously belonged to the patrimony of the alienator.[90]
Acquisition by particular title is the acquisition of one or more particular assets which previously belonged to someone else.[91] According to art. 3:80 § 3 BW 'property is acquired by particular title by transfer, prescription, expropriation and in any other manner of acquisition of rights provided by law according to their kind'.[92] In the case of acquisition by particular title the acquirer generally does not have to respect the personal obligations of the transferor with respect to the object. However, Dutch law recognizes the exception of the qualitative obligation, which is a contractual stipulation pertaining to registered property, which ensures the devolution of certain personal obligations to tolerate or refrain from certain Actions upon persons who subsequently acquire that property by particular title, or who subsequently acquire a personal or residual right upon that property (art. 6:252 § 1 BW). Moreover, the law obliges the transferee to respect certain personal obligations. For example, the acquirer has to respect tenancy agreements (art. 7:226 BW, the enactment of the famous principle *emptio non tollit locatum*) and lease agreements (art. 34 Farm Lease Act (*Pachtwet*)).[93]
The acquisition by particular title *by transfer* could be the result of a diversity of obligations. Usually the obligation to transfer will arise from a synallagmatic (obligatory) contract, such as sale, barter, gift or partnership, or from a contract by gratuitous title like a gift (*schenking*, the subject of Book 7 Title 3 BW). The obligation to transfer could also follow from a unilateral legal act, such as a

---

[86] *Asser-Mijnssen-De Haan* 3-I, p. 155.
[87] Art. 4:182 in conjunction with art. 3:80 § 2 BW.
[88] Art. 1:93 and 1:94 BW.
[89] Art. 2:309 in conjunction with 3:80 § 2 BW.
[90] *Asser-Mijnssen-De Haan* 3-I, p. 155 and 156.
[91] *Asser-Mijnssen-De Haan* 3-I, p. 156.
[92] A form of derivative acquisition by particular title of a movable not explicitly mentioned by art. 3:80 § 3 BW occurs when a thing is delivered on a resolutive condition. Where delivery is made in the performance of a conditional obligation, the right so acquired is subject to the same condition as the obligation (art. 3:84 § 4 BW). Thus, the asset is transferred to the acquirer in the case of a delivery on a resolutive condition. But the moment when the condition is fulfilled, the conditional right returns to the transferor. This is a derivative acquisition of the right as it belonged to the person to whom it was delivered on the resolutive condition.
[93] *Asser-Mijnssen-De Haan* 3-I, p. 155.

legacy. Furthermore, the obligation could stem from the law:[94] for example, the obligation to contribute all gifts, received from the deceased, to the estate (art. 4:229 BW), the obligation to return by transfer after undue payment of a thing,[95] or the obligation to undo the performances which have already been made at the time of the fulfilment of a resolutory condition.[96] A very important legal obligation to transfer is found in art. 6:271 BW:

> *The setting aside of a contract liberates the parties from the obligations affected by it. To the extent that these obligations have already been performed, the legal ground for this performance remains intact, but an obligation arises for the parties to undo the prestations which they have already received.*

A tort (unlawful act) is another important example of a legal obligation which functions as a valid title for transfer (i.e. the transfer of a thing by way of the payment of damages).[97] The same applies to the obligation to pay damages in case of unjustified enrichment (art. 6:212 BW). It is debated, however, whether the payment should be regarded as damages, but this does not need to concern us here.

Finally, the obligation to transfer could arise from a more complex legal relation, i.e., the obligation to transfer could arise from two of more successive obligatory contracts between parties other than those between whom the transfer needs to take place, the so-called ABC contracts.[98] See for this subject below, Section 7.

5.3.2. Defects regarding the obligation and their effects on the transfer of ownership

The validity of the transfer and the validity of the real agreement effectuating it depend upon the validity of the underlying contract (doctrine of causality), witness the requirement of 'delivery pursuant to a valid title' (art. 3:84 § 1 BW). The legal act underlying the title could be void or annulled, or in case the legal act underlying the title is a contract, this contract could be terminated.

---

[94] HR 17-11-1967, NJ 1968, 42 (*Pos/Van den Bosch*).

[95] Art. 6:203 § 1 BW: *A person who has given property to another without legal ground is entitled to reclaim it from the recipient as having been paid unduly.*

[96] Art. 6:24 § 1 BW: *After fulfilment of a resolutory condition, the creditor must undo what has already been performed, unless the content or the necessary implication of the juridical act produce a different result.*

[97] See HR 18–6-1971, NJ 1971, 408.

[98] Pitlo-Reehuis, *Goederenrecht*, p. 82.

5.3.2.a. Void or annulled titles

The title could prove to be void from the beginning. The title could also be annulled prior to delivery or after delivery has taken place. As annulment 'has retro
active effect to the time the juridical act was executed' (art. 3:53 § 1 BW), the annulled title is considered to be void from the beginning.

Legal acts are *void* in the following cases:

- The legal act has not been performed in the prescribed form (unless the law produces a different result); art. 3:39 BW.
- The legal act is by its content or necessary implication contrary to good morals or public order
- The legal act constitutes a violation of an imperative statutory provision (unless the provision is intended solely for the protection of one of the parties to a multilateral juridical act, in which case the act may only be annulled and provided that the necessary implication of the provision does not produce a different result. Statutory provisions which do not purport to invalidate juridical acts which are contrary to them, are not affected by this rule; see art. 3:40 BW.
- The legal act was performed by an incapable person and was unilateral, provided it is not addressed to one or more specifically determined persons; see art. 3:32 BW.

Legal acts are *annullable* in the following cases (the enumeration is not complete):

- The legal act was performed by a person who lacked legal capacity (art. 3:32 BW, see above),
- The legal act was performed by someone whose mental faculties are permanently or temporarily impaired, provided it is unilateral and not addressed to one or more specifically determined persons; see art art. 3:34 BW,
- The legal act was entered into as a result of a threat, fraud or abuse of circumstances; see art. 3:44 BW,
- The legal act was entered into as a result of an error (mistake); see art. 6:228 BW,[99]

[99] The German concept of *Irrtum über die Zahlungsfähigkeit* (error concerning the solvency of the other party) is not known in Dutch law. Error concerning the person of the other party in general, however, is recognized and even put on an equal footing with other kinds of errors (examples of error concerning the person: mistaken identity, error concerning the religion, the morality, the profession, the abilities etc. of the other party). I have not been able to find any court decision in which a contract was annulled because one of the parties had incorrect ideas about the solvency of

- The legal act (contract) was in furtherance of an already existing juridical relationship between the parties: the act can in principle be annulled if this relationship does not exist; see art. 6:229 BW,
- The legal act was harmful to the creditors of the alienator (*Actio Pauliana*); see art. 3:45-48 BW and art. 42 Bankruptcy Act (*Faillissementswet*).

In the case of a void, or prior to or after delivery annulled, title the transfer is (in the latter case in hindsight) based upon an invalid title. Consequently, the transfer is invalid and the transferor is still the owner of the asset, provided he was the owner to begin with.[100] This is the essence of the principle of causality. However, art. 3:53 § 2 BW provides that

> *the judge may, if so demanded, refuse to give effect to an annulment in whole or in part, if the juridical act has already produced effects which can only be undone with difficulty. He may order that a party who is prejudiced by his decision be compensated by a party who unjustly benefits from it.*

The *Travaux Préparatoires* of the BW indicate that this power of the judge is to be used only in exceptional cases.[101] Moreover, in case of abuse of circumstances and influence of error the judge has the power to adapt – instead of nullify – the contract under special circumstances. Art. 3:54 § 2 BW provides that

> *instead of pronouncing the annulment for abuse of circumstances, the judge may, upon the demand of one of the parties, modify the effects of the juridical act to remove this prejudice.*

Similarly, art. 6:230 § 2 BW provides that in the cases meant in art. 3:228-229 (see above: contracts entered into as a result of error or contracts in furtherance of an already existing juridical relationship between the parties in case this relationship does not exist)

> *instead of pronouncing the annulment the judge may, upon the demand of one of the parties, modify the effects of the contract to remove this prejudice.*

In those instances a valid title for transfer remains. Furthermore, the transferor and the transferee are entitled to confirm the validity of the void or avoidable transfer (art. 3:58 BW).

---

the other party. The possibility to annul a contract on that basis would, in my opinion, be an unjustified infringement on the *paritas creditorum*,and would furthermore be at odds with the possibility to exercise the right of revendication (art. 7:39 BW, see below § 5.7) or to stipulate another security instrument like a reservation of title, which is nothing other than a safeguard against the insolvency of the other party.

[100] The retroactive effect of annulment is irrelevant if the alienator was, for example, a thief.

[101] *Parl. Gesch*. Boek 3, p. 239.

5.3.2.b. Obligations which do not constitute valid titles for transfer

Art. 3:84 § 3 BW mentions two kinds of obligations which do not provide a valid title for transfer:

> *A juridical act which is intended to transfer property for purposes of security or which does not have the purpose of bringing the property into the patrimony of the acquirer after transfer, does not constitute a valid title for transfer of that property.*

The purpose of the provision – usually referred to as the *prohibition on fiduciary transfer (fiduciaverbod)* - is to guarantee the restricted system of absolute rights by preventing ownership or another right from being divided into absolute rights other than those recognised by law. The provision has been widely debated (most authors recommend its removal from the BW) and in 1995 the *Hoge Raad* chose to adopt a restricted interpretation of its purposes.[102]
Art. 3:85 BW mentions two other obligations which do not provide a valid title for transfer. However, by operation of law those obligations are converted into obligations which do provide a valid title for transfer. Art. 3:85 § 1 BW provides that

> *an obligation which is intended to transfer property for a certain specific period is deemed to be an obligation to establish a usufruct upon the property during that specific period.*

And the second paragraph of this article provides that

> *a obligation which is intended to transfer property under a suspensive term is deemed to be an obligation to transfer the property immediately, and establishes simultaneously a usufruct upon the property in favour of the alienator during the relevant period.*

The latter provision has been criticized as an infringement on the autonomy of the parties, as the alienator intended to give up his ownership but the law forces him to maintain ownership on behalf of the other party, who, contrary to his wishes, does not receive ownership but (merely) the right of usufruct.

5.3.2.c. Termination of a contract

The termination of a contract does not have retroactive effect (art. 6:269 BW). Neither does the termination of the contract return the ownership of the asset to the transferor by operation of law. This is because the termination of the contract does not affect the title as it existed at the moment of the transfer. The termination of the contract brings about a new obligation – which forms a statutory title – for

[102] *Asser-Mijnssen-De Haan* 3-I, p. 212. See HR 19-5-1995, NJ 1996, 116 (*Sogelease*).

the acquirer to return (retrotransfer) the asset to the transferor (art. 6:271 BW). Thus, the original alienator only has a personal claim against the acquirer of the asset, the weakness of which manifests itself if the acquirer is declared bankrupt before the performance of the obligation to retrotransfer the property.
The situation is different in the case of the fulfilment of a resolutive condition of a contract. Like termination, the fulfilment of a resolutive condition does not have retroactive force (art. 3:38 § 2 BW). But, as said before, where delivery is made in the performance of a conditional obligation, the right so acquired is subject to the same condition as the obligation (art. 3:84 (4) BW). Thus the conditional right returns to the transferor by operation of law at the moment when the condition is fulfilled. The same applies to the assertion of the right of revendication by the seller of a movable (art. 7:39 BW): ownership returns to the seller automatically, but without retroactive force. If the buyer has already transferred the property for value to a third acquirer in good faith before the seller asserted his right of revendication, the third acquirer is protected by art. 7:42 BW (note that this transfer was made by someone who was entitled to dispose of the property, as the subsequent revendication has no retroactive effect; the protection of art. 3:86 is therefore not applicable).

5.4. Tradition

5.4.1. Dogmatic basis

In the new code of 1992, the principle of publicity is maintained as a cornerstone of property law, in which legal certainty is crucial in view of the *drittwirkung* of absolute rights. Above, in § 1.2.1, two examples are given of provisions in the field of transfer where the importance which the Dutch legislator still attaches to the principle is visible: transfer of movables requires the transfer of possession and assignment of claims requires notice thereof to the debtor (however: since October 2004 another form of assignment has been introduced, in which a claim may be transferred without notice to the debtor. The principle of publicity is not abandoned here, however, for this kind of assignment has to be performed by an authentic deed or a registered deed under private writing).
Obviously, the principle of publicity is frequently under pressure, especially due to the rise of (relatively) new instruments in the field of finance and security: fiduciary transfer, financial leasing, factoring, securitisation, etc.: examples of phenomena in which outsiders cannot tell who owns the objects they are confronted with.[103] Publicity has, so far, not been sacrificed, even though the

[103] In the first two examples, there is a separation of legal ownership and economic ownership. Factoring and securitisation are both characterized by the fact that the person collecting payments from the debtors of the claims involved is not the eventual beneficiary of the payment (in the case

legislator is not averse to facilitating the new instruments (witness the just mentioned introduction of 'silent assignment' for the benefit of factoring and securitisation). The Europeanization of Dutch law plays a role too: in the implementation legislation concerning the Collateral Directive of the EU the prohibition on fiduciary transfer (art. 3:84 § 3 BW) has been excluded for repos.
Principles are always balanced against other principles. Many provisions of property law are the result of a compromise between publicity and the need to favour and promote undisturbed trade. Therefore, it is not possible to assess the 'effectiveness' of the rules which require publicity: the ultimate goal of the legislator is not publicity in itself, but the simultaneous advancement of the diverse principles at stake to some kind of optimum.

5.4.2. Forms of tradition

As said, the concept of delivery is regarded as consisting of two elements: (1) the real agreement and (2) the act by which the transferor and the transferee manifest their common intention to transfer. The law prescribes certain formalities for the manifestation of the common intention to transfer. Art. 3:39 BW provides that 'unless otherwise provided by law, legal acts, which are not performed in the required form, are void'. Thus, if those formalities are not observed, delivery is void. Consequently, the transfer is void (art. 3:84 § 1 BW).
The formalities required for a transfer vary according to the kind of asset to be transferred. The formalities required for the transfer of movables differ with respect to (a) movables which are in the power of the transferor, (b) movables which are not in the power of the transferor and (c) movables which are registered objects[104].

5.4.2.a. Movables which are in the power of the transferor

Art. 3:90 § 1 BW provides that 'delivery required for the transfer of movables which are unregistered property and which are in the power of the alienator is made by providing possession of the thing to the acquirer'. The article applies only where the transferor has power over the thing. The term power in this article means direct possession (actual physical power) as well as indirect possession (power through a detentor). There are different ways in which possession may be provided (see also above, § 2.3).

---

of securitisation it is customary for the originator to maintain responsibility, as the servicing agent, to collect the payments of the claims).
[104] Certain ships and aircraft.

5.4.2.a.1. Actual tradition

Art. 3:114 BW provides that

> *a possessor transfers his possession by enabling the acquirer to exercise such control over the property as he himself was able to exercise over it.*

The simplest way to provide possession is the handing over of the object, e.g. a bicycle could be delivered by handing over the bicycle. But possession could also be provided by any other act which gives direct possession over the object according to common opinion. Such an act could be the handing over of objects giving direct possession over the object, e.g. the bicycle could also be delivered by handing over the keys (*traditio symbolica*). Or such an act could be the permission of the transferor to the transferee to take possession of the object, e.g. the bicycle could be delivered by taking the bicycle out of the bicycle-rack.[105] Such other act (than the handing over of the object) should not be regarded as a separate kind of fictitious tradition. For if it gives the acquirer direct control over the object in question, it is actual tradition. 'Whether somebody detains property and whether he does so for himself or for another, is determined according to common opinion, taking into account the following rules and, otherwise, the facts as they appear' (art. 3:108 BW).

5.4.2.a.2. Fictitious tradition

Art. 3:115 BW provides that

> *a bilateral declaration without material acts is sufficient for the transfer of possession:*
>
> *(a) where the alienator possesses the thing and henceforth detains it for the acquirer by virtue of a stipulation made at the time of delivery;*
>
> *(b) where the acquirer was detentor of the thing for the alienator;*
>
> *(c) where a third party detained the thing for the alienator and detains it for the recipient after the transfer. In the last event possession does not pass until the third party has acknowledged the transfer or has been notified of it by the alienator or acquirer.*

In short, art. 3:115 BW defines the *constitutum possessorium* (a), the *traditio brevi manu* (b) and the *traditio longa manu* (c).

Constitutum possessorium (art. 3:115 (a) BW) is defined as the form of tradition where the transferor is the possessor of the thing and the parties agree that the transferor will henceforth hold the thing for the transferee as a detentor. As the object remains in the hands of the transferor, a transfer constitutum possessorium

[105] Pitlo-Reehuis, *Goederenrecht*, p. 182.

is 'invisible' to third parties. Because of this infringement of the principle of publicity the effect of such a transfer is restricted. This is effected in two provisions: art. 3:90 § 2 BW (with regard to transfer constitutum possessorium by a possessor) and art. 3:111 BW (with regard to transfer constitutum possessorium by a detentor):

Art. 3:90 § 2 BW provides that delivery of a thing which remains in the hands of the alienator has no effect with respect to a third person who has a prior right to the thing, until the time when the thing has come into the hands of the acquirer, unless the third person has consented to the alienation.

Art. 3:111 BW provides that a person who has begun detention for another pursuant to a juridical relationship continues to do so under the same title, so long as no change is apparent in his title which results either from an act by the person for whom he holds or from the latter's right having been contested. Consequently, a detentor of an asset cannot, in principle, turn or 'intervert' his detention into possession, nor can he turn his detention for a certain person into detention for another.[106]

Both provisions are based on the argument that a transferee who does not insist on acquiring actual power over the object involved, does not deserve the normal third party protection against the transferor lacking the privilege to dispose, as long as he leaves the object involved in the hands of the transferor.[107] The difference between the two provisions is that art. 3:90 § 2 BW nullifies the transfer constitutum possessorium only as against third parties having an older right in the object, whereas art. 3:111 BW nullifies the transfer of possession entirely.

In the case of *traditio brevi manu* (art. 3:115 (a) BW) the asset to be delivered is already held by the transferee. Thus, whereas a *traditio constitutum possessorium* turns the possessor (transferor) into a detentor, tradition *brevi manu* turns the detentor (transferee) into a possessor.

The *traditio longa manu*[108] (art. 3:115 (a) BW) is a form of tradition which covers the situation in which the asset to be transferred is in the custody of a third person. The third party does not have to agree with the change in possession. To be valid the *traditio longa manu* should either be assented to by the detentor or notified to him. As notification suffices the third party is unable to block the transfer of possession. Without or even against his will his detention for the transferor will be changed into detention for the acquirer. However, he will retain all contractual rights he had against the transferor.

---

[106] The rule that a detentor cannot turn himself into a detentor for a third person has been clearly expressed in HR 22-5-1953, NJ 1954, 189 (Sio/De Jong), HR 29-9-1961, NJ 1962, 14 (*Smallingerland/Picus*) and HR 8-6-1973, NJ 1974, 346 (*Nationaal Grondbezit/Kamphuis*). See Van Vliet, *Transfer of movables*, p. 146.

[107] Van Vliet, *Transfer of movables*, p. 145. See *Parl. Gesch.* Boek 3, p. 384-385.

[108] NB: The modern use which Dutch law makes of the term *traditio longa manu* does not correspond with the term's original meaning. Van Vliet, *Transfer of movables*, p. 142-143.

Although a detentor cannot transfer ownership by way of *constitutum possessorium* (due to the prohibition of interversion of art. 3:111 BW), he is able to transfer ownership by way of *traditio brevi manu* or *traditio longa manu*. A detentor does not have the power to dispose, but this defect could be rectified by art. 3:86 BW, which protects the transferee in good faith against a transferor's lack of privilege to dispose of movables which were in the power of the transferor.[109] Neither does the detentor possess the thing. Therefore, he is not able to *transfer* possession to the acquirer. However, art. 3:90 § 1 BW does not require the 'transferor' to *transfer* possession, but merely to *provide* possession. This covers all instances of transfer of possession, but includes cases in which a *detentor* provides another with the actual power over a thing. In the latter case the transferee will originally acquire possession of the thing, as a result of occupation. Therefore, it is said that the acquirer has been provided with the possession of the thing, although there has been no *transfer* of possession. Thus, a factual handing over of the object by a detentor is sufficient to meet the requirement of art. 3:90 § 1 BW. Strictly speaking, fictitious tradition (as meant in art. 3:114 BW) is not available to a detentor, because it is a form of transferring *possession*. However, a detentor may provide possession in a way resembling *traditio brevi manu* or *traditio longa manu* as long as it gives the acquirer the power over the thing required by art. 3:90 § 1 BW. Providing possession in a way resembling *constitutum possessorium* is not sufficient, because in that case the actual power remains with the transferor.[110]

Sometimes a fourth form of fictitious tradition is recognized: *traditio sine manu*. The term, which is not mentioned in the civil code, is used to indicate the tradition between two people living together, married or unmarried. If a husband makes a gift of furniture to his wife, any physical act of moving the furniture is unnecessary. Art. 3:114 BW does not fit this situation, for the husband does not provide his wife with the power he previously had over the furniture. His physical power over the things remains intact and his wife already had the same physical power before the transfer of possession.[111] See above, § 2.3.

The agreement mentioned in art. 3:115 BW is not the real agreement, but the agreement on the transfer of possession. The requirement of providing possession should be distinguished from the legal act of transfer, the real agreement, whether the provision of possession takes place by way of actual of fictitious tradition. The transfer of possession – actual of fictitious – needs an agreement. But this agreement is solely about the transfer of possession and it is therefore not

[109] See § 5.1.3.
[110] Van Vliet, *Transfer of movables*, p. 147.
[111] Van Vliet, *Transfer of movables*, pp. 143-144.

identical to the real agreement, which is an agreement about the transfer of ownership rather than possession.[112]

A special form of transfer is the transfer through the delivery of **documents** in which ownership of goods is 'embodied': *bills of lading, warehouse warrants* etc. Documents like these are made in the form of bearer documents or order documents. See on the delivery of these documents art. 3:93 BW:

> *Delivery required for the transfer of a right payable to bearer, the instrument of which is under the control of the alienator, is made by delivery of the document in the manner and with the effects as specified in articles 90, 91, and 92. The same applies to the transfer of a right payable to order which is under the control of the alienator, provided that the document is also endorsed.*

In the document, the carrier or depositary declares what he will deliver the (movable) goods concerned to the bearer or order of the documents. In this way, transfer of possession is effected through the transfer of the documents, and thereby also the transfer of ownership (art. 3:90 § 1 BW).[113]

See on warehouse warrants art. 7:607 (in the Title on Deposit), and on bills of lading art. 8:399 and 8:916 BW (Book 8 is titled Traffic and Transport). Other forms of documents of title, recognised in Book 8 BW are the *Delivery order* (document issued by the carrier after the withdrawal of the bill of lading, which entitles the bearer of the document to the delivery of the goods mentioned in the bill of lading; art. 8:482) and the *CT document* (art. 8:44 ff.).

In all these provisions, the 'technique' is the same: the delivery of the document *before* the delivery of the goods mentioned therein counts as the delivery of these goods. This implies that the transfer of the goods by delivery of the goods themselves (instead of the document) remains a possibility if the document has not (yet) reached the addressee.[114]

5.4.2.b. Movables which are not in the power of the transferor

Art. 3:90 § 1 BW requires the transferor to provide the acquirer with possession of the thing for the transfer of a movable. All forms of tradition involve a transfer of possession, and accordingly a derivative acquisition of possession. But when the thing is not within the power of the owner, for example as a result of theft, the owner cannot provide possession. However, there is a practical need to be able to

---

[112] Van Vliet, *Transfer of movables*, p. 137.

[113] See Snijders/Rank-Berenschot, *Goederenrecht*, § 243, and especially A.J. van der Lely, *Levering van roerende zaken door middel van een zakenrechtelijk waardepapier* (Thesis, Groningen 1996).

[114] Nevertheless, if a bill of lading has been issued only the rightful bearer is entitled to demand delivery of the goods vis-à-vis the carrier (art. 8:940 BW).

transfer ownership in these instances, especially to the insurance company (insurance policies usually make payments in the case of theft conditional upon the transfer of the ownership of the stolen object). Therefore, art. 3:95 BW enables the owner to transfer ownership by drawing up a deed. This deed contains the mutual will to transfer the ownership of the thing, that is, the real agreement. Art. 3:95 BW provides that 'in cases other than those provided for in articles 89 – 94 and without prejudice to articles 96 and 98, property is delivered by a deed intended for that purpose'.

5.4.2.c. Movables which are registered objects

Pursuant to art. 3:89 § 4BW, movable registered property is delivered in the same manner as immovable things (the provisions of § 1-3 apply *mutatis mutandis*). This means that a notarial deed intended for that purpose has to be drawn up between the parties, followed by its entry in the public registers provided for that purpose. This applies to registered sea vessels and river craft (art. 8:199 § 1 and art. 8:790 § 1 BW), registered aircraft (art. 8:1306 § 1 BW) and any encumbered rights on these things (hypothec, usufruct etc.).

5.5. Registration

There are only two categories of movables of which the transfer is effected (constitutively) through registration: certain ships (registered sea vessels and river craft, art. 8:199 § 1 and art. 8:790 § 1 BW) and certain aircraft (registered aircraft, art. 8:1306 § 1 BW): see above, § 5.4.2.c. They constitute movable registered property (*Registered property is property the transfer or creation of which requires entry in the public registers, provided for that purpose*; art. 3:10 BW). Motor vehicles are not registered property, even though the transfer of vehicles is registered:[115] when one buys a car (or motorcycle), one must transfer the vehicle registration certificate to one's own name. This registration is not constitutive, however: the transfer of ownership is effected independently of compliance with the registration requirement.

5.6. Real agreement

The concept of a real agreement is not undisputed in Dutch law. Whereas the different formalities required for the transfer of assets are clearly laid down in the civil code, the real agreement is neither mentioned in the old nor in the new civil code. Especially with respect to the delivery of non-registered movables by actually handing them over the opinions differ on the meaning of (and the

[115] By the Government Road Transport Agency (*Rijksdienst voor het wegverkeer*).

practical need for) the real agreement.[116] Some jurists maintain that the transfer of possession is not a legal, but a factual act, and that therefore no place is left for a real agreement. Others argue that even delivery by actual handing over implies a transfer of possession (legal act), which accordingly implies a real agreement.[117] Nevertheless, the concept of a real agreement is acknowledged by a majority of Dutch legal authors.[118] They contend that the requirement of a real agreement is implied by the fact that the transfer of property is not brought about by the obligatory agreement, but by a separate legal act (delivery).[119] Besides, the *Travaux Préparatoires* indicate that the law starts from the concept of real agreement[120] and the *Hoge Raad* has recognised the real agreement[121] as an element of delivery in several decisions.[122]
In order to be effective the real agreement should relate to a specific good. This follows from art. 3:84 § 2 BW which provides that 'the title must describe the property in a sufficiently precise manner'. The unfortunate term 'title' in this paragraph does not refer to the obligation to transfer, but to the real agreement (the execution of the obligation to transfer).[123] According to art. 6:227 BW 'the obligations which parties assume must be determinable'. 'Determinable' in art. 6:227 BW means that criteria, if necessary subjective criteria, could be found for determining the subject matter of the obligation.[124] This is broader than 'sufficiently precise' in the meaning of art. 3:84 § 2 BW[125], which means that objective criteria could be found, if necessary subsequently, for determining

[116] See on this Drobnig: "The validity of the real agreement depends upon the validity of the underlying contract as its *causa* (doctrine of causality). This causal nature of the real agreement is unanimously accepted in Dutch literature (...). The real agreement is completely integrated into the contractual context since its existence and validity is on a par with all other contractual clauses. It only differs as to its effect, since these are proprietary and not contractual. The Dutch controversy about the real agreement therefore is purely conceptual, without practical relevance, except where the Civil Code expressly provides for it." U. Drobnig, 'Transfer of Property', in: *Towards a European Civil Code*, 2nd ed., Nijmegen, 1998, p. 507.
[117] P.C. Slangen, *Hoofdstukken Goederenrecht* (3rd ed; The Hague 2002), pp. 24-25.
[118] See for a survey *Asser-Mijnssen-De Haan* 3-I, p. 167.
[119] *Asser-Mijnssen-De Haan* 3-I, p. 166.
[120] *Parl. Gesch.* Boek 3, p. 380; *Parl. Gesch.* Boek 6, p. 837; *Parl. Gesch.* Boek 3 (Inv. 3, 5 and 6), p. 1250.
[121] N.B.: Under the old Dutch civil code the real agreement was called *zakelijke overeenkomst*. Under the new Dutch civil code it is referred to as *goederenrechtelijke overeenkomst*.
[122] HR 7-6-1946, NJ 1946, 465; HR 29-9-1961, NJ 1962, 14; HR 18-2-1966, NJ 1967, 109; HR 24-5-1968, NJ 1969, 72; HR 8-3-1972, NJ 1973, 482; HR 8-6-1973, NJ 1974, 346; HR 27-4-1979, NJ 1981, 139; HR 1-2-1980, NJ 1981, 140; HR 7-5-1982, NJ 1983, 241.
[123] *Asser-Mijnssen-De Haan* 3-I, p. 174-175; O.K. Brahn and W.H.M. Reehuis, *Overdracht, Monografieën Nieuw* BW B6a,(3rd ed.; Deventer 1997), pp. 42-43.
[124] Brahn/Reehuis, *Overdracht,* p. 41.
[125] Brahn/Reehuis, *Overdracht* , pp. 41-43.

which object is to be, or has been, transferred.[126] Therefore, the term 'title' in art. 3:84 § 2 BW refers to the moment when the obligation to transfer, which results from the title, will be effectuated, i.e. the moment of delivery.[127]
Besides, this follows from the 'principle of individualisation'. Ownership of unascertained goods cannot exist and as a consequence generic goods cannot be transferred unless it is known exactly which individual assets are to pass to the acquirer. If an obligation exists for the transfer of a certain number of generic goods, which will be specified later on, the appropriation of those goods must take place in the real agreement. The real agreement has the role of specifying the assets and thus of complying with the principle of specificity.
An invalidity, which affects the real agreement, only prevents the purported performance of the transferor's obligation to transfer the property to the transferee. But his obligation as such is not affected The transferor remains obliged to transfer and must make a new attempt to transfer the property or else he will be burdened with the consequences of his non-performance. This, of course, is the main argument of the 'adversaries of the real agreement': the annulment of a delivery (e.g. on the basis of a threat, art. 3:44 BW) is futile because it merely postpones the delivery: eventually the obligation to deliver will have to be performed.

5.7. Payment – right of revendication

As has been said above (§ 5.2), Dutch law does not recognize a requirement of payment for the acquisition by transfer based upon a sales contract. This means that there is no implied reservation of title, as is the case in Belgium. However, in the interests of salesmen art. 7:39 BW gives the seller the right to reclaim unpaid goods (right of revendication or right of recovery). See art. 7:39 § 1:

> *The seller of a movable thing (not registered property) which has been delivered to the buyer, is entitled, in case the price has not been paid and thereby the conditions for termination ex article 265 Book 6 have been fulfilled, to reclaim the thing by a written declaration addressed to the buyer. By this declaration the sale is dissolved and the right of the buyer or his legal successor ends (...).*

The importance of the right of revendication lies in its proprietary effect: ownership returns automatically to the seller, whereas the ordinary termination of the contract would merely create a personal obligation for the buyer to transfer the thing back to the seller. In its legal effects, the right of revendication is

[126] Brahn/Reehuis, *Overdracht*, pp. 41-43; HR 20-6-1997, NJ 1998, 362; HR 19-9-1997, NJ 1998, 698; HR 19-12-1997, NJ 1998, 690.
[127] *Asser-Mijnssen-De Haan* 3-I, p. 174-175; Brahn/Reehuis, *Overdracht*, pp. 42-43.

comparable to the transfer under a resolutory condition (see above, § 5.3.1): both lead to an automatic return of title but without retrospective effect.
The term of forfeiture of this special right is specified in art. 7:44 BW: the right ends when both six weeks have passed since payment became due and 60 days have passed since the day on which the thing was stored by the buyer or someone on his behalf. Usually, therefore, the right ends 60 days after actual delivery. Third persons who in the meantime have acquired a right on the thing are protected by art. 7:42, provided they have acquired their right for value and they reasonably could not have expected that the seller would exercise his right of revendication.

6. Double selling

When A sells the same asset first to B and afterwards also to C, both B and C are entitled to delivery. For this situation art. 3:298 BW gives priority (with exceptions) to the claim by B:

> *Unless the law, the nature of their rights or the requirements of reasonableness and equity*[128] *produce a different result, where two or more creditors pursue conflicting rights to delivery in respect of one and the same property, the oldest right to delivery has preference in their mutual relationship.*

This provision is only relevant if seller A does not perform voluntarily. If, however, A does deliver voluntarily, either to B or to C, art. 3:298 has no role to play. B (if A had delivered to him) or C (*idem*) will acquire ownership, as the last requirement for transfer has been fulfilled by the delivery. Good faith is not required.
Under certain circumstances the other party will be entitled to hold him liable: this will be the case if the buying of the thing constituted an unlawful act, because he knew that it had already been sold to someone else. The possibility of a condemnation to transfer the thing to the other party is recognized by the *Hoge Raad*.[129]
Even if the acquirer did not know at the time of the sale that the seller had already sold the object to someone else, but he learned about that fact before the delivery, he can under special circumstances be successfully accused of an unlawful act.[130]

[128] Example: B has bought a house for reasons of speculation, without the intention to live in the house himself, while C has bought the same house in a desperate need for a place to live. In that case, C's right of delivery of C would have preference over the right of B because of the requirements of reasonableness and equity (See W. Snijders, "Botsende rechten op levering van eenzelfde goed", in: *Recht door zee, Liber Amicorum H. Schadee* (Zwolle 1980), pp. 185-192).
[129] HR 17-11-1967, NJ 1968, 42 (*Pos/Van den Bosch*).
[130] See HR 8-12-1989, NJ 1990, 217.

With regard to the *double delivery of future goods,*[131] art. 3:97 § 2 BW provides the following:

> *Delivery in advance of future property has no effect against a person who has acquired the property in advance as a result of an earlier delivery. In the case of a movable thing, the delivery has effect against this person from the time the thing has come into the hands of the acquirer.*

In the second sentence, the subordination of the delivery constitutum possessorium (see art. 3:111 and 3:90 § 2 BW, discussed in § 2.3 and 5.4.2.a) and the importance of the principle of publication is yet again expressed: whoever succeeds in acquiring actual control of the thing will prevail. If that is the person to whom the thing was delivered last (B), there is a further problem. The delivery through which he obatined control of the thing has effect against the other party (A), but that does not imply that he automatically becomes the owner: the seller was no longer entitled to deliver the thing to B, as A had already acquired ownership. In other words, the seller no longer had the right to dispose of the thing. Therefore B will also be in need of protection against the fact that the alienator was not entitled to dispose of the thing: this protection will be awarded to him if he is in good faith (meaning that he did not know nor ought to have known that A had already acquired ownership) and his acquisition was not gratuitous (see art. 3:86 § 1 BW).

7. Selling in a chain

7.1. The notion of combined title

As said above, in § 5.1.2 and 5.1.3, the title which is required for a valid transfer (art. 3:84 § 1 BW), is defined as 'the legal relationship which underlies and justifies the transfer'. The express purpose of this definition, introduced by A.S. Hartkamp in 1974, is to cover cases like the one in which A sells to B and B sells to C, after which A delivers directly to C. Transactions of this type are called ABC contracts, and the underlying title is considered to be a 'combined title' (*samengestelde titel*).[132, 133]

---

[131] With the exception of registered property and property which cannot be the subject matter of a contract, future property may be delivered in advance; art. 3:97 § 1BW.

[132] See *Asser-Mijnssen-De Haan* 3-I, no. 239, S.E. Bartels, *De titel van overdracht in driepartijenverhoudingen* (Thesis; Utrecht 2004) and A.S. Hartkamp, 'De samengestelde overdrachtstitel en zijn manco's', *WPNR* 6596 (2004), pp. 849-856.

[133] In all these cases it seems obvious that the 'real agreement' constituting the delivery A-C is concluded between A and C, and that B is not a party to that agreement. However, the matter has drawn hardly any attention from Dutch scholars, so it is not possible to construe a common opinion.

In the following situations a combined title is present:[134]

- *ABC contracts*: A sells to B and B sells to C, after which A delivers directly to C (mentioned above);

Indirect agency: A transfers a movable to B, who acts as an indirect agent (*middellijke vertegenwoordiger*) for C and accepts the movable on behalf of C (see art. 3:110 BW and below);

- *Assignment*: A sells to B and B sells to C, after which A delivers to C after assignment by B to C of his right to delivery by A;
- *Third Party Clause*: A delivers to C after C has accepted a Third Party Clause in the contract A-B to that effect;
- *Takeover of a debt*: A delivers to C after A has taken over B's obligation to C;
- *Takeover of a contract*: B transfers to C his position as the buyer in the sales contract A-B.

7.2. Defects in either of the two relationships

In the code of 1992, no attention is given to the consequences of defects in either the relationship A-B or the relationship B-C.[135]
In cases in which there is a defect in the relationship A-B, the protection of C is possible by analogous application of articles 3:86 and 3:88 BW: these provisions protect the bona fide purchaser who acquires a non domino (art. 3:86 applies to movables, art. 3:88 to immovables, other registered property and claims). Both rules are not directly applicable, because there is no separate transfer B-C, but analogous application seems appropriate.[136]
In cases in which there is a defect in the relationship B-C, the protection of A is possible in view of art. 6:34 BW:

> *A debtor who has paid a person who was not entitled to receive payment, can invoke his release by payment against the person to whom the payment should have been made, if he had reasonable grounds to believe that the recipient of the payment was entitled to the performance as creditor or that payment was to be made to him for another reason.*

[134] See Hartkamp, 'De samengestelde overdrachtstitel', p. 850.
[135] This is the same for Dutch and for Austrian law (both causal tradition systems): doctrine is responsible for the acknowledgement of the combined title. Reportedly, in Austrian law C is protected against a defect in de relationship A-B (by § 367 ABGB), but there is no protection for A if there is a defect in the relationship B-C (according to Bartels and Hartkamp).
[136] See in favour of this solution especially Hartkamp, 'De samengestelde overdrachtstitel', p. 852.

After A has delivered to C (as B had instructed him to do so), A is discharged from his obligations, despite the defect in the relationship B-C. But what about the ownership of the property? In the end, the property should belong to B, as the relationship between him and C was made defective and C therefore ought to return the property to B. This can be achieved by allowing B to claim the property from C on the basis of art. 6:36 and/or 6:212. Art. 6:36 provides that the person who in reality is entitled to payment has recourse against a person who has received payment without having a right thereto.[137] Art. 6:212 provides that a person who has been unjustifiably enriched at the expense of another must, to the extent that this is reasonable, make reparation for the damage suffered by that other person up to the amount of his enrichment.[138]
If *both* relationships (A-B and B-C) are made defective simultaneously, the property will have to return to A. C is not protected by (the analogous application of) the abovementioned provisions for lack of good faith, and B would have no recourse to art. 6:212 against C (or A) because there would be no unjustified enrichment of C (or A) at the expense of B. There would not even be a valid combined title, as both constituent titles are invalid. A would still be owner.

7.3. Acquisition through someone else (e.g. indirect agency)

In art. 3:110 BW, a special rule is given for acquisition through someone else (e.g. an indirect agent). The provision has been quoted and discussed above, in § 3.4, to which I refer. In short, art. 3:110 provides that C (the principal in an agency-setting) automatically becomes the possessor of the property which B (the agent of C) acquires on his behalf from A. With regard to movables, this has the effect that the principal acquires ownership, as the delivery of movables is effected by the transfer of possession (art. 3:90 § 1). In other words: ownership is directly transferred from A to C (with the effect that the bankruptcy of B is not an obstacle).

---

[137] This only applies in cases referred to in articles 6:34 (quoted above) and art. 6:35 (§ 1: *Where payment made by a third person fulfils, with respect to that person, the requirements of either of the paragraphs of the preceding article, the third person can invoke the releasing force of that payment in his favour.* § 2: *The debtor can invoke the releasing force of that payment in his own favour if, through his own payment, he would also with respect to himself have complied with those requirements.*

[138] See again Hartkamp, 'De samengestelde overdrachtstitel', p. 853. Hartkamp does not discuss the complication that for the application of art. 6:212 it is required that the enrichment of C was at the expense of B. When the relationship A-B was gratuitous, this is not the case, and so art. 6:212 BW offers no solution in such a case.

8. Insolvency of the transferor or acquirer

8.1. Contracts and bankruptcy

In principle, a bankruptcy order does not influence existing contracts or the rights and obligations they entail, unless a legal exception exists. The Bankruptcy Act

(*Faillissementswet*) contains three such exceptions: arts. 37, 39 and 40. The last two provisions deal with lease and labour contracts, and can be left aside here.
Art. 37 Bankruptcy Act deals with the situation in which a synallagmatic contract has not or only partially been fulfilled by both the debtor and the other party at the time of the bankruptcy order. The trustee in bankruptcy is to declare within a reasonable period, granted to him in written form by the other party, whether he is prepared to fulfil the agreement. If the trustee declares that he is prepared to fulfil the agreement, he is obliged to furnish security along with that declaration (art. 37 § 2).
If, on the other hand, the trustee does not do so in time, or he declares that he is not prepared to fulfil the agreement, he loses the right to demand the fulfilment of the contract by the other party (art. 37 § 1 Bankruptcy Act). The other party is then entitled to dissolve the contract and claim damages: he may come in as a creditor in bankruptcy with this ordinary debt (art. 37a). In this way, the claim is treated as if it had arisen before the bankruptcy order,[139] which is justified by the fact that it has taken the place of the one which had indeed arisen by then).

8.2. Actio Pauliana (in bankruptcy)

Dutch law acknowledges the so-called Actio Pauliana both outside (invoked by the trustee) and inside (invoked by individual creditors) bankruptcy settings. The 'Pauliana outside bankruptcy' has been discussed above, in § 5.3.2 (and briefly in 3.2). Below, I will only discuss the 'bankruptcy Pauliana.'[140]
If a Dutch curator decides to annul[141] one of the bankrupt's legal acts on the basis of its Paulianic nature (that is: harmful to his other creditors), then he has to state

[139] See art. 24 Bankruptcy Act: the bankrupt's estate is not obliged to meet the obligations of the debtor, arisen after the bankruptcy order, unless (and as far as) it had profitted from it.
[140] A.M.J. van Buchem-Spapens and Th.A. Pouw, *Faillissement, surseance van betaling en schuldsanering*. Monografiën Privaatrecht 2 (Deventer 2004), *Ch. V (* p. 41-49). The following survey has for a large part been borrowed from A.F. Salomons, "Dutch case note; Hof van cassatie van België/Cour de cassaton de Belgique, 31 January 2002 – The effect of annulment in bankruptcy as against a third party acquirer in good faith", *European Review of Private Law* 6-2004, pp. 804-809.
[141] This sanction differs from that in, e.g., Belgium: in Dutch law Paulianic legal acts are avoidable, while in Belgian law they are non-invokable against the estate of the bankrupt. As far as I can see, this makes no great difference: in either case it is (in the Netherlands *de iure*, in Belgium

and if necessary prove that the next four conditions have been fulfilled (art. 42 § 1 and 2 Bankruptcy Act):

1. the legal act must have been non-obligatory,[142] meaning that there was no (legal or contractual) duty to perform this act. Annulment is impossible in case of an obligatory performance of a legal act, unless either the other party knew that bankruptcy had already been filed or the debtor and creditor had the joint intention to favour this creditor above the other creditors (art. 47).[143]
2. The interest of the creditors must have been harmed:[144] the size of the bankrupt's estate must have been diminished.[145]
3. It has to be proven that the debtor knew or ought to have known that the interests of the creditors would be harmed.[146]
4. In the case of a legal act other than by gratuitous title it must also be proven that the other party knew or ought to have known that harm to the creditors' interests would occur.

Whether these last two conditions have been fulfilled is difficult to prove. For that reason, art. 43 Bankruptcy Act determines that knowledge of the prejudice is assumed on the side of both the debtor and the other party in the case of a legal act mentioned in the article, performed within a year before the bankruptcy order, provided that the debtor had not before that period committed himself to perform

---

de facto) up to the curator to decide whether to take the Paulianic nature of the legal act into account, or to let matters rest.

[142] In Dutch: *onverplichte rechtshandeling*. In case of giving in payment - performing in another way than was due - this condition is fulfilled: a legal act like this has to be considered non-obligatory, as the debtor is not *obliged* to make this kind of performance, notwithstanding the fact that he is *entitled* to perform in this manner if he has the permission of the creditor (see art. 6:45 of the Dutch Civil Code). Art. 6:45 indicates that giving in payment has to be considered the performance of the *original* obligation, and not as novation (substitution of one debt for another). Novation would require the waiving of the original claim by the creditor. See on this Asser-Hartkamp, *Verbintenissenrecht* 4-I (11th ed., Deventer, 2000), no. 625. This is established case law and *communis opinio* among the authors. For case law see especially HR 18-12-1992, *NJ* 1993, 169 (*Kin Emmerig q.q.*) and HR 20-11-1998, *NJ* 1999, 611 (*Verkerk/Tiethoff q.q.*). With regard to the legal literature I refer for brevity only to F.M.J. Verstijlen, 'Het onverplichtheidsvereiste bij de (faillissements)Pauliana', *Tijdschrift voor Insolventierecht* 1999/6, pp 127-131, with further references.

[143] Knowledge of the prejudice to the interests of the other creditors is not sufficient here: intention is required. See HR 24-3-1995, *NJ* 1995, 628 and HR 20-11-1998, *NJ* 1999, 611.

[144] In Dutch: *benadeling van schuldeisers*.

[145] See HR 19-10-2001, *NJ* 2001, 654. This has to be determined, not at the moment when the legal act was performed, but the moment when the curator invokes the Actio Pauliana or - in case of legal proceedings - the moment when the judge decides. HR 22-3-1991, NJ 1992, 214 (*Loeffen q.q.-Mees en Hope II*): the fact that creditors are merely missing out on some benefit does not imply that their interests have been harmed.

[146] In Dutch: *wetenschap van benadeling*.

the legal act. Furthermore, knowledge of prejudice is assumed on the side of the debtor in the case of a legal act by gratuitous title, performed within a year before the bankruptcy order; art. 45 Bankruptcy Act.

This complex set of rules can be summarized as follows: the curator is entitled to annul a legal act if he states and if necessary proves that it was non-obligatory, causing prejudice to the creditors and of which the debtor (and in case of a legal act other than for gratuitous title also the other party) knew or ought to have known that it would cause this prejudice. In the cases specified in articles 43 and 45 Bankruptcy Act knowledge of the fact that the legal act causes prejudice is assumed. Annulment of an exigible debt is possible only if it is proven that the receiver knew that bankruptcy proceedings against the payer were instituted or that the payer and receiver had conspired in order to favour the latter above the other creditors.

The third-acquirer in good faith is protected against the annulment by the trustee pursuant to art. 51 § 2 Bankruptcy Act, which reads as follows:

> *Rights, acquired by third persons in good faith and under onerous title, are respected. There is to be no reclaim from a third person who has acquired in good faith and by gratuitous title, in so far as he proves that he had not benefited from the legal act at the moment of the bankruptcy order.*

This provision is a *lex specialis* for third party protection in the context of the Actio Pauliana in bankruptcy. So the general provision on the protection of the acquirer in good faith and under onerous title of movables (art. 3:86 BW) does not apply here.

This is relevant for the position of the acquirer by gratuitous title: he can never invoke art. 3:86, but the protection of art. 51 § 2 Bankruptcy Act is available to him, provided that he did not benefit from the legal act. Art. 3:45 § 5 BW contains an almost identical rule for the Actio Pauliana in a non-bankruptcy setting; in that case, too, the annulment does not have effect against a third acquirer in good faith and by gratuitous title, in so far as he proves not to have benefited. There is only a difference with regard to the moment at which the presence or absence of benefit has to be determined: for the 'bankruptcy *Pauliana*', this is the moment of the bankruptcy order, for the 'ordinary' *Pauliana* the moment when the acquired object is reclaimed.

8.3. Insolvency of the transferor

8.3.1. Bankruptcy between sale and delivery

If a transferor is declared bankrupt after the title of transfer (e.g. a sales contract) has come into being but before delivery has taken place, the acquirer is not 'protected' against the general creditors of the transferor: Art. 35 Bankruptcy Act determines that a delivery can no longer be performed if not all of the acts, required for a delivery by the debtor, have taken place on the day of the bankruptcy.[147] The principle behind art. 35 is that the bankrupt's estate should remain intact for the benefit of the creditors who are entitled to recover their claims from that estate.[148] Obviously, art. 35 is a mandatory rule of law, as it aims to protect other parties.

The consequence of art. 35 is that the acquirer is not in a strong position: he has a personal right to delivery, which counts as an ordinary debt, to be presented to the trustee in bankruptcy for the creditors' meeting.

If the delivery/acquisition takes place after the bankruptcy order, but before the order is published,[149] the acquirer has recourse to the protection of the bona fide acquirer a non domino of art. 3:86,[150] provided that it is established that he was indeed in good faith. After the publication, those who have acquired from the bankrupt are considered to have known the fact that the transferor lacked the right to dispose: art. 35 § 3 Bankruptcy Act. Art. 35 § 3 Bankruptcy Act does not apply to registered property: the acquirer of such property is not protected on the basis of his good faith when the delivery was completed before the publication of art. 14 Bankruptcy Act, as long as the bankruptcy was entered in the Bankruptcy Register; see art. 3:24 § 2 under c BW.[151]

With regard to future goods:[152] if the debtor has delivered a future good in advance before his bankruptcy and the good is acquired[153] by him after he was declared bankrupt, then the transfer has no effect: the good forms part of the bankrupt's estate: see art. 35 § 2 Bankruptcy Act.

---

[147] See HR 14-7-2000, NJ 2001, 685 on assignment: if the assignor had made and signed the deed of assignment before he was declared bankrupt, but the debtor of the claim had not yet been notified, the assignment cannot be completed afterwards by performing the notification at a later date: the claim remains part of the bankrupt's estate and if the trustee in bankruptcy wishes the assignment to go ahead, he has to make a new deed of assignment, followed by notification (see art. 3:94; the introduction of silent assignment had not yet taken place in 2000).

[148] Van Buchem-Spapens/Pouw, *Faillissement, surseance van betaling en schuldsanering,* p. 29.

[149] Pursuant to art.14 § 3 Bankruptcy Act publication is required in the Netherlands Government Gazette (*Nederlandsche Staatscourant*) and in one or more newspapers.

[150] The same applies to the protection of art. 3:238 BW for a pledge.

[151] See Van Buchem-Spapens/Pouw, *Faillissement, surseance van betaling en schuldsanering,* p. 33.

[152] Van Buchem-Spapens/Pouw, *Faillissement, surseance van betaling en schuldsanering,* p. 24. The extensive and complex case law on the assignment of future claims can be left aside here, as our subject is the transfer of movables.

[153] Goods acquired by the bankrupt at the result of inheritance form part of the bankrupt's estate (art. 20 Bankruptcy Act). The trustee in bankrupcy is entitled to decide whether an inherinance is accepted or renounced; art. 41 Bankruptcy Act; see Van Buchem-Spapens/Pouw, *Faillissement, surseance van betaling en schuldsanering*, p. 25.

If an indirect agent is declared bankrupt before the delivery of a movable thing, acquired for the principal, the latter is protected by the special provision of art. 3:110 BW. This provision has been discussed above in § 3.4, 7.1 and especially 7.3, to which I refer. In short, the principal acquires ownership ipso facto, despite the bankruptcy of the agent.
As art. 35 Bankruptcy Act is mandatory, direct deviation is not possible.[154] Nevertheless, it is possible to regulate by contract what the effects of a declaration of bankruptcy of either of the parties will be on the contract. Take, for example, a loan: usually a loan contract stipulates the immediate exigibility of the remaining debt in the case of the bankruptcy of the borrower. This is relevant to the amount of the claim to be allowed by the trustee in bankruptcy.[155]

8.3.2. Bankruptcy after transfer under suspensive condition

In the case of transfer under a suspensive condition, the bankruptcy of the transferor before the fulfilment of the condition does not obstruct the acquisition by the transferee. This follows from art. 3:84 § 4 BW:

> *Where delivery is made in the performance of a conditional obligation, the right so acquired is subject to the same condition as the obligation.*

This means that the delivery under suspensive condition has led to the acquisition of a 'conditional right':[156] whether the acquirer will eventually receive ownership depends *only* on the fulfilment of the condition: the fact that the transferor by that time has lost the right to dispose is irrelevant.[157] The fulfilment of the condition has no retroactive effect (art. 3:38 § 2 BW), so ownership passes from the transferor to the transferee at a stage when the bankruptcy of the former has already set in.

8.3.3. The position of the transferee in the case of delivery on the basis of an invalid sale

If a sales contract is *terminated (*dissolved*)* after delivery to the transferee, the latter is obliged to undo the performance he has already received, and the same applies to the seller (art. 6:271 BW[158]). This means that the buyer is obliged to

---

[154] Otherwise, there would be no need for phenomena like the reservation of title.
[155] Van Buchem-Spapens/Pouw, *Faillissement, surseance van betaling en schuldsanering*, p. 39.
[156] I mention only in passing here that some authors reject the notion of 'owner under suspensive condition' because it suggests that the acquirer already is, in a way, the owner, whereas in reality he is not. See above, § 3.2.
[157] See Pitlo-Reehuis, *Goederenrecht*, no. 125.
[158] Art. 6:271: *The dissolution of a contract liberates the parties from the obligations affected by it. To the extent that these obligations have already been performed, the legal ground for this*

redeliver the acquired property to the seller. If the seller has been declared bankrupt, the buyer is entitled to suspend this obligation, as he can reasonably expect that he will not (or not immediately) obtain restitution of the price he has paid. This right of suspension (art. 6:52/262BW), which implies a right of retention (art. 3:290 BW), can also be invoked against the creditors of the seller (art. 6:53), which includes the trustee himself.[159]

The picture is different in the case of an *annulment* of the sales contract: as an annulment has proprietary effect, ownership returns to the seller with retroactive effect (art. 3:53 BW). The buyer is left with the possession of the property. If he is to be regarded as possessor in good faith, he has a right of retention, but only for the obligation of the seller to reimburse him for the costs expended on the property, as well as for the damages for which the possessor might be liable toward third persons by reason of his possession; see art. 3:120, discussed above (§ 1.4.2. and 1.6.1.).

8.4. Insolvency of the transferee

In a tradition system like the Dutch BW, the position of the seller in the case of the bankruptcy of the buyer is primarily determined by whether or not delivery has already taken place: if it has, ownership has passed to the buyer and the seller is – unless some special protective provision is available, see below – left with a mere personal claim if payment by the buyer is still due.

The most important exception to this general rule is to be found in the law of sales: the seller is equipped with the proprietary protection of art. 7:39 (right of revendication), which was discussed above in § 5.3.2. (under *Termination of a contract*) and was quoted in § 5.7. In short: in case of non-payment by the buyer the seller is entitled to dissolve the sales contract in written form, as a consequence of which ownership returns to the seller ipso facto without retroactive effect. Pursuant to art. 7:44 BW, this right of revendication ends when both six weeks have passed since payment became due and 60 days have passed since the day on which the thing was stored by the buyer or someone on his behalf. In contrast to this protection of the seller is a rather generous protection of third persons who have acquired rights on the sold property in good faith before the right of revendication was exercised; art. 7:42 BW.

If the title of transfer is *annulled* after delivery to the transferee – either by the transferor, the transferee or a third party (e.g. the trustee in bankruptcy) – the transferor regains ownership (annulment has retroactive effect; see above, § 8.3.)

---

performance remains intact, but an obligation arises for the parties to undo the prestations which they have already received.

[159] See *Parl.Gesch.* Boek 6, p. 211.

and is entitled to revendicate[160] the property from the transferee, whether the latter has been declared bankrupt or not. If the annulment takes place before delivery, the transferor is liberated from the obligation to transfer ownership to the transferee and therefore to deliver the thing to him. The bankruptcy of the transferee is therefore without any consequence. [161]

Again, the *termination* (dissolution) of the contract from which the title of transfer stems – because of the non-performance of either transferor or transferee – presents a different picture, because of the fact that termination has no proprietary effect. If delivery has preceded the termination, ownership remains with the transferee, who is merely obliged to redeliver the thing to the transferor (art. 6:271 BW). If the transferee is bankrupt, the thing forms part of the bankrupt's estate and the trustee is free to proceed towards execution; the personal claim of the transferor to undo the transfer is not an obstacle to this.

If delivery has not taken place at the moment when the contract is terminated, the situation is, from a proprietary viewpoint, similar to that of the annulment of the contract before delivery: the transferor is still the owner of the property and is liberated from the obligation to deliver it to the transferee, so that the bankruptcy of the latter is without consequence.

It case of traditio by *constitutum possessorium* ownership passes to the transferee before the thing is actually handed over to him. In that case, annulment leads to a return of ownership to the transferor (theoretically, possession is still in the hands of the transferee, but due to the fact that the transferor now starts to possess the thing for himself once again one can discern that he "contests" the right of the transferee; this leads, pursuant to art. 3:111 BW, to a return of possession to the transferor; see above, § 1.2.1., 2.3. and 5.4.2.a.). Termination does not have this effect, so that the bankruptcy of the transferee still leaves the latter with the ownership of the property, even though this is still in the hands of the transferee. Obviously, the latter is entitled to suspend his obligation to hand it over to the transferee, as he has the personal right of art. 6:271 to the retrodelivery of the property by the transferee.[162]

---

[160] This revendication of the owner of a thing (art. 5:2 BW) is not to be confused with the just mentioned right of revendication (in Dutch: *reclamerecht)* of the seller of a movable thing (art. 7:39 BW). One of the important differences is that the revendication of art. 5:2 is subject to a limitation period of 20 years, whereas the right of revendication of art. 7:39 expires in a couple of weeks.

[161] Unless the judge makes use of the exception under art. 3:53 § 2 BW: *The judge may, if so demanded, refuse to give effect to an annulment in whole or in part, if the juridical act has already produced effects which can only be undone with difficulty. He may order that a party who is prejudiced by his decision be compensated by a party who unjustly benefits from it.*

[162] With regard to movables, delivery is effected by the giving of possession (art. 3:90 § 1 BW, see above, § 1.2.1, 5.4.2.a and *passim*), that is: enabling the acquirer to exercise control over the property (art. 3:114 BW). If delivery is made through a middelman (a carrier), it depends on the contractual setting whether possession passes at the moment when the property is presented by the

In case property is transferred under *resolutive condition* (e.g. a title reservation), the acquirer receives ownership which is to end ipso facto by the fulfilment of the condition; see art. 3:84 § 4 BW (quoted above in § 8.3.). This also applies if that fulfilment of the condition (in the case of title reservation usually payment by the transferee) takes place after the latter is declared bankrupt: ownership of the acquired thing leaves the bankrupt's estate and returns to the transferor.
An exception to the above has to be made for cases in which the transferee has acquired ownership by accession, specification or confusion of goods which had previously been transferred to him (see below, Section 10). This is the case when he processes the acquired goods in the manufacture of new goods. These forms of original acquisition imply that the ownership of the goods which had been transferred to him ceases to exist; this renders the return of ownership (in the case of annulment) or the coming into existence of a claim for retrodelivery (in the case of termination) of the transferred goods impossible. The transferor is left with a claim arising from the contract or from unjustified enrichment. The bankruptcy of the transferee is irrelevant: the original acquisition occurs due to the manufacture itself, irrespective of any (lack of) entitlement on the part of the manufacturer.

9. The passing of risk and proprietary interests in the property

9.1. Transfer of movables and the passing of risk

With regard to the passing of risk, the BW provides rules only in the context of sales contracts (Book 7 Title 1 BW). Art. 7:10 § 1 and 4 read as follows:

> 1 *The thing is at the risk of the buyer as of the delivery, even if ownership has not been transferred. As a consequence, the purchase price remains owed irrespective of the loss or deterioration of the thing by a cause which cannot be imputed to the seller.*
>
> 4 *Where, after delivery, the thing has remained at the risk of the seller, the seller is also responsible for the thing's loss or deterioration by the act of the buyer. However, as of the time when the buyer must reasonably foresee that he must give the thing back, he is obliged to look after the safekeeping of the thing as a prudent debtor (...).*

---

transferor to the middelman or at the moment when it is presented by the middelman to the transferee: it is decisive under whose instructions the middleman operates (who has called the middleman in?). If it is the transferor under whose instructions the middleman operates, the former is in a position to instruct the middleman to abort the delivery if he learns that the transferee is probably not going to fulfill his obligations. It seems that this would result in a similar situation as *stoppage in transitu* (a legal concept which in itself is alien to Dutch law).

The notion of delivery (in Dutch *aflevering*, not to be confused with *levering*, even though both words have to be translated as delivery) in art. 7:10 § 1 refers to art. 7:9 § 2, in which delivery (*aflevering)* is defined as 'putting the buyer into possession of the thing.'

Art. 7:10 § 1 BW is in accordance with art. 69 CISG and art. 97 LUVI. By following these regimes, the Roman Law principle of *periculum est emptoris* has been abandoned. The French system, in which the risk passes to the buyer at the moment when ownership is transferred, has the disadvantage that it does not place the risk in the hands of the person who has actual control of the thing (in the consensual French system even less so than in the Dutch tradition system): the person who has control of the thing is the obvious person to burden with the obligation to take care of the preservation of the thing.[163]

Art. 7:10 BW is non-mandatory. In the case of a consumer sale,[164] however, there may be no derogation to the detriment of the buyer. Furthermore, art. 7:11 BW provides:

> *If, in a consumer sale, the seller or a carrier designated by him delivers the thing at the buyer, the thing is only at the risk of the buyer as of that time, even if it had already been delivered in the sense of article 9.*

It should be prevented that the buyer could postpone the passing of the risk by not cooperating in the delivery. Therefore, art. 7:10 § 2 BW determines that the risk also passes in such a case of the creditor's default:

> *The same [as provided in art. 7:10 § 1, quoted above, A.F.S.] applies as of the time when the buyer is in default of performing an act by which he must cooperate in the delivery. In the case of sale of things determined as to kind, the default of the buyer does not transfer the risk to him until the seller has specified the thing destined for the performance of the contract and has notified the buyer thereof.*

If, on the other hand, the seller would be late in delivering (the debtor's default), this would only result in the postponement of the passing of the risk, as this would have passed earlier if he had performed on time.

---

[163] See Asser-Hijma 5-I, *Koop en ruil* (5th ed.; Zwolle 1994), no. 509. Compare art. 6:27 BW*: A person who is obliged to deliver a thing certain and determinate must care for it until delivery, in the manner in which a prudent debtor would do so in the circumstances.*

[164] A consumer sale means the sale of a movable thing entered into by a seller acting in the course of a business or profession, and by a buyer who is a natural person not acting in the course of a business or profession; art. 7:5 § 1 BW.

9.2. The passing of the various interests in the property

With regard to the passing of the *right to dispose of the property* and *the right to exercise the remedies of ownership*: these interests pass (in principle) at the moment when ownership passes. Under certain circumstances it is possible to transfer the right to dispose before the passing of ownership takes place. The most obvious example is the sales contract in which a reservation of title is stipulated, combined with a clause that entitles the buyer to dispose of the property before the fulfilment of the condition that ends the ownership of the seller (normally: payment by the buyer).[165] That the right of revendication passes with the ownership of the thing concerned, is clear from the words of art. 5:2 BW: revendication is awarded to "the owner of a thing". Nevertheless, in several cases a remedy similar to that of the owner is awarded to non-owners. See for an example art. 3:295, which provides that a creditor who loses control of the thing can reclaim it under the same conditions as an owner in order to re-establish his right of retention (see above, § 2.4). Another example is art. 3:125 BW, which entitles the person who has acquired possession of property to institute, on the basis of a subsequent loss of or disturbance in the possession, the same Actions against third persons to recover the property and to remove the disturbance as the title-holder of the property.
With regard to the *right to the fruits* of the property, the basic rule is that fruits belong to the owner of the thing from which the fruits are separated; see art. 5:1 § 3 BW:

> *Without prejudice to the rights of others, the owner of the thing becomes owner of the fruits once separated.*[166]

However, when the thing is not in the hands of the owner, but with a possessor in good faith, the latter is entitled to the fruits (art. 3:120 § 1 BW):

> *Separated natural fruits and civil fruits which have become exigible betlong to the possessor in good faith.*

In that case, the acquisition of the possession is decisive and therefore the moment of the delivery equally so.

---

[165] See on the subject of disposing of the property of someone else in general L.Groefsema, *Bevoegd beschikken over andermans recht* (thesis; Deventer 1993).

[166] This rule should be read in combination with art. 5:17, which attributes fruits to the usufructuary, the leaseholder etc.: *The person who, pursuant to his right of enjoyment of a thing, is entitled to its fruits acquires the ownership thereof upon their separation.* When the property is not encumbered with such a right of enjoyment, the owner of the thing is himself entitled to the fruits (upon their separation).

Part III: Original acquisition

10. Accession, confusion and specification

10.1. Terminology: component part and principal thing

Art. 3:4 § 1 BW provides that anything which, according to *common opinion*, forms a part of a thing is a **component part** of that thing. For example: a key is, according to common opinion, a component part of the lock and a keyboard is regarded as component part of a computer. Furthermore, a thing which is attached to a principal thing in such a manner that it cannot be separated therefrom without substantial damage being done to either, becomes a component part of that thing, pursuant to § 2 of art. 3:4 BW.

Component parts do not have an independent proprietary existence; their legal status depends on the legal status of the principal thing. This implies that the owner of a thing to which another thing becomes a component part, acquires the ownership of that part. This is provided for in art. 5:14 (accession of movables), art. 5:15 (confusion) and 5:16 (specification) and 5:20 BW (accession of movables by immovables).[167] These provisions will be discussed in detail below.

Art. 5:14 provides that a thing is deemed to be a **principal thing** where its value considerably exceeds that of the other thing, or where, according to common opinion, it is considered as such.

In an illuminating case, the *Hoge Raad* has decided that a machine does not become a component part of the building by the mere fact that it plays an important role in the production process of the factory in that building: what matters is common opinion about the relationship between the building and the machine: is the building in its construction especially equipped for the machine and does the building (as a factory building in general) have to be regarded as *unfinished* as long as the machine is missing?[168] So the relation between the things themselves is crucial, not their function or role. An elevator is a good example of a machine which, according to this rule, would be a component part of the building if they were constructed to be joined together: the building would have to be regarded as unfinished without its elevator.

[167] See especially J.E. Wichers, *Natrekking, vermenging en zaaksvorming. Opmerkingen bij de algemene regeling voor roerende zaken in het Burgerlijk Wetboek.* Serie Recht en Praktijk 121 (Thesis; Deventer 2002).

[168] See HR 27-11-1992, NJ 1993, 317 (*Zaaimachine*) and Pitlo-Reehuis, *Goederenrecht,* no. 12.

10.2. Accession of movables

The first paragraph of 5:14 BW provides:

> *1. The ownership of a movable thing which becomes a component part of another movable thing, which itself is to be regarded as the principal thing, passes to the owner of the principal thing.*

This rule implies that no accession (in Dutch: *natrekking*) occurs when neither of the things involved is to be regarded as the principal thing or component part. If, for example, two more or less equal movables are combined to constitute a new thing (two short plastic tubes are glued together to form a longer tube) the process cannot be called accession, and the basic rule of § 1 does not apply. The process does have proprietary effect, however, if the constituent parts of the new thing had different owners. This effect is specified in § 2: the owners become its co-owners, each for a share proportionate to the value of the thing:

> *2. If none of the things can be regarded as the principal thing, and if they belong to different owners, these owners become co-owners of the new thing, each for a share proportionate to the value of the thing.*

It follows that the two constituent parts do not have to be entirely equal or have exactly the same value for this provision to apply, but if the value of one of them *considerably* exceeds that of the other thing that thing would be deemed to be the principal thing (art. 5:14 § 3, discussed above in § 10.1) and its owner would acquire ownership of the new thing. As long as neither thing has a value that considerably exceeds that of the other thing(s) and common opinion does not regard either thing as the principal part, no accession occurs and ownership of the new thing is shared proportionate to the value of the constituent thing(s).

10.3. Confusion

According to art. 5:15 BW, the preceding article on accession (art. 5:14) applies *mutatis mutandis* where movable things belonging to different owners are amalgamated so as to form a single thing. This refers to the process of confusion (in Dutch: *vermenging*): the mingling of substances or things which cannot be individualized amongst themselves: water is added to wine, two gasses are joined, two loads of potatoes are stored together etc. Whether or not a chemical reaction occurs, is irrelevant, but the process should not involve any creative work, as the process would then count as specification (art. 5:16 BW).[169]

Art. 5:15 applies only if one of the constituent things is a component part and another the principal thing (according to the criteria of art. 3:4 BW) and the constituent things belonged to different owners. If, for example, a sugar cube

[169] See Pitlo-Reehuis, *Goederenrecht*, no. 514.

belonging to A is thrown into the cup of tea belonging to B, B would become the owner of the new thing 'tea-with-sugar' (the cup of tea would be the principal thing, according to both the criteria of art. 3:4, common opinion and the different values). If two similar things are mingled (e.g. two loads of flour), there will be no principal thing according to common opinion, so the different values of the two loads will be decisive: if the value (in this case this is the same as: quantity) of one load considerably exceeds that of the other, then there is a principal thing and a component part, and therefore confusion occurs.
Confusion has to be distinguished from the phenomenon which in Dutch literature is called **improper confusion:** the process by which things which can be individualized become mixed up. This occurs when cars, animals, machinery with registration numbers, stock, numbered bank notes etc. are mingled.[170] Confusion does not occur in these cases, so the mingling has no proprietary effect. The only legal effect the process may have is that the owners of the different objects are not able to prove which things are theirs, and so they will not succeed in revendicating their belongings. This problem does not belong to the realm of Property law, but to that of the Law of evidence.
The leading case in this field is HR 12-1-1068, NJ 1968, 274 (*Teixeira de Mattos*): different owners had deposited four depositary receipts for shares with a bank, which became bankrupt. In the bankrupt's estate only four depositary receipts were found, but in the past the receipts had been part of a constantly changing stock portfolio and their numbers had not been noted. The depositors were not entitled to revendicate the four receipts as they were unable to prove that these four receipts were the same receipts as they had deposited.[171]

10.4. Specification

As in the case of accession and confusion, through specification (in Dutch: *zaaksvorming*) a new thing is created. In this case, the creative process is crucial: it has to be an *essentially new* thing: the "design" has to be so important that the value of the new thing is, for a large part, made up by it[172]. Examples are the creation of a valuable work of art out of a couple of pipes of limited value by a sculptor or of a culinary masterpiece out of some ordinary ingredients by a chef. Because of the emphasis on the creative element in the coming into existence of the new thing (in this context sometimes called a *novum*), the proprietary

---

[170] The examples are given by Pitlo-Reehuis, *Goederenrecht* no. 516.

[171] This problem no longer occurs due to the arrival of book-entry securities which are characterized by giro-transfer: see Pitlo-Reehuis, *Goederenrecht* no. 516 and Snijders/Rank-Berenschot, *Goederenrecht*, no. 171.

[172] *Parl. Gesch* Boek 5., p. 109.

consequences differ from those of accession or confusion. The basic rule, however, is the same; see art. 5:16 BW:

> *1 If a person creates a new thing out of one or more movable things, this thing is owned by the owner of the original things. The two preceding articles apply mutatis mutandis where these things belonged to different owners.*

In principle, therefore, the creator acquires the ownership of the new thing only if he was the owner of the original things. If he was not, the new thing is acquired by the owner of the original things, and if there were different owners one has to differentiate: if a principal thing and component part can be distinguished, the owner of the principal thing becomes the owner of the newly created thing, otherwise the original owners acquire co-ownership proportionate to the value of their thing.

Paragraph 2 provides an exception when the specification took place for the specificator himself: he acquires ownership of the new thing, whether or not he was the owner of the original things, provided the costs of creation[173] justify this outcome:

> *2 If a person creates a thing for himself, or has such a thing so created in whole or in part out of one or more movable things not belonging to him, he becomes owner of the new thing, unless the costs of creation are so low as not to justify this result.*

Obviously, this is a very important provision: industrial manufacturing, for example, involves specification on a massive scale. The effect of the provision is that reservation of title is not a useful security instrument in the transfer of raw materials or semi-finished products: if the acquirer uses them in a way that constitutes specification, all previous rights on them expire due to the original acquisition by the specificator.[174]

For the application of § 2 it is not important whether the specificator creates the new thing himself or has someone else to do so for him. This is logical: the owner of a factory will not perform the specification himself, but will leave the actual creative process to the workers of the factory. The process, however, takes place on his behalf.

According to the third paragraph, the first two paragraphs apply mutatis mutandis to the transformation of materials into a new material or to the cultivation of plants. An example of 'transformation of materials' is the processing of raw

---

[173] Costs of labour included. The *Hoge Raad* decided (in HR 5-10-1990, NJ 1992, 226 (*Breda/St. Antonius*)) that for the question of who acquires ownership by the specification the limited value of the used materials compared to the labour costs is in principle irrelevant.

[174] See especially O.K. Brahn, *Toelevering van voorwerpen onder eigendomsvoorbehoud bij industriële fabricage volgens huidig en komend recht* (Deventer 1984).

petroleum into petrol and other products of which the combined value is many times greater than that of the orignal petroleum.[175] Similar examples can be given for the manufacturing processes in the pharmaceutical industry.
The cultivation of plans out of seeds, seedlings or cuttings is also considered specification.[176] A case law example is to be found in HR 5-12-1986, NJ 1987, 745 (*Gescheurde orchideeën*) on the tearing in two of orchids. The cultivation of orchids is performed by separating them into two parts, each of which is a new plant. The *Hoge Raad* acknowledged that this process implied specification of new plants: the tearing is an irreversible process by which new plants come into being with their own separate lives and with, according to common opinion, their own identities, different from the identity of the original plant. This implied that the reservation of title with regard to the original plants expired.

10.5. Accession of movables by land

Article 3:3 BW defines as immovable: land, unextracted minerals, plants attached to land, *buildings and works durably united with land,* either directly or through incorporation with other buildings or works. Pursuant to the second paragraph of the article, all things which are not immovable, are movable.
The proprietary counterpart of this provision is to be found in art. 5:20 BW under e BW:

> *To the extent not otherwise provided for by law, ownership of land comprises:*
> *a. the surface;*
> *b. the layers of soil under the surface;*
> *c. subsoil water which has surfaced by means of a spring, well or pump;*
> *d. water which is on the land and not in direct connection with water on the land of another person;*
> *e. buildings and works durably united with the land, either directly or through incorporation with other buildings or works, to the extent that they are not component parts of an immovable thing of another person;*
> *f. plants united with the land.*

From the provision under e we can conclude that buildings and works durably united with the land have to be seen as component parts of the land. From that moment on, they are dependent parts of the immovable they are united with.
Whether or not an object is durably united with the ground is an issue that is frequently taken to court. In the so-called Portacabin case[177] the *Hoge Raad* ruled

---

[175] *Parl. gesch.*,Boek 5, p. 109.
[176] *Parl. gesch.* Boek 5, p. 110.
[177] HR 31-10-1997, NJ 1998, 97 (*Ontvanger/ Rabobank*).

that an object is immovable, provided it is, with regard to its nature and layout, intended to be durably united with the ground. If this is the case it does not matter whether it is technically possible to move the object easily or not. In determining whether the object is meant to be durably united with the ground, it is necessary to look at the knowable intentions of the constructor of the object or the person who has commissioned it.

The important Portacabin ruling has been much discussed since 1997, and many new cases have found their way to court (on harbour cranes, on sea containers, on tombstones[178], etc.). Criticism of the ruling focuses on the fact that the Portacabin criterion (an object is immovable if it is intended to be durably united with the ground) leaves no room for common opinion (except to determine the occurrence of 'durability' and 'to unite'), as the *Hoge Raad* explicitly stated.

The occurrence of the vertical accession of art. 5:20 BW under e can be prevented by the establishment of a *right of superficies* (art 5:101 BW). This enables the superficiary "to own or to acquire buildings, works or plantations in, on or above an immovable thing belonging to another."

Accession is also prevented when a *legal exception* has been made, as is expressed in the opening words of art. 5:20 BW. This has been done with regard to telecom cables in the Telecommunication Law: the Telecom company retains the ownership of the cables it has laid in the land belonging to others. The *Hoge Raad* recently decided in a (tax) case involving similar cables that a cable network is an immovable object (again: pursuant to the Portacabin criterion), even though the process of burying cables into the ground does not lead to accession due to the legal exeption to the rule of art. 5:20 BW in the Telecommunication Law.[179]

11. Bona fide purchase (acquisition a non domino)

See for the system of third party protection in Dutch property law in general above, § 5.1.3. In this section only the protection of the acquirer a non domino of

[178] HR 25-10-2002, NJ 2003, 241 (*St. Barbara/Aartsbisdom Utrecht, Grafsteenarrest*). Tombstones are durably united with the cemetery, so (purusant to the Portacabin criterion), the owner of the cemetery is the owner of the tombstones therein. This is not altered by the fact that common opinion awards ownership of a tombstone to the family members who have ordered and placed the stone, the fact that most tombstones do not have a foundation and graves are cleared away after a couple of decades, the fact that most cemeteries prefer to leave the ownership to those family members (if only to avoid liability for possible damage caused by the tombstones) as is usually expressed in the general terms and conditions, used in their contracts.

[179] HR 6-6- 2003, BR 2003/9 (*CAI*).

a movable thing, unregistered property, provided in art. 3:86 BW, will be discussed.[180] Art. 3:86 provides:

1. *Although an alienator lacks the right to dispose of the property, a transfer pursuant to articles 90, 91 or 93 of a movable thing, unregistered property, or a right payable to bearer or order is valid, if the transfer is not by gratuitous title and if the acquirer is in good faith.*

2. *Where property mentioned in paragraph 1 and having been transferred, otherwise than by gratuitous title and according to articles 90, 91 or 93, is encumbered with a dismembered right which the acquirer does not know nor ought to have known at the time of the transfer, this right is extinguished; in the case of a transfer according to article 91, the extinction is subject to the same suspensive condition as the delivery.*

3. *Nevertheless, the owner of a movable thing, who has lost its possession through theft, may revendicate it during a period of three years from the day of theft, unless*

   a) the thing has been acquired by a natural person, not acting in the exercise of a profession or business, from an alienator whose business it is to deal with the public in similar things, otherwise than at a public sale, on business premises destined for that purpose, being an immovable structure or part thereof with the land belonging thereto, and provided that the alienator be in the ordinary exercise of his business; or

   b) money or documents payable to bearer or order are involved.

4. *Articles 316, 318 and 319 regarding the interruption of the prescription of a right of Action apply mutatis mutandis to the period referred to in the preceding paragraph.*

11.1. Field of application

Art. 3:86 applies whenever a movable thing, unregistered property is transferred by someone who lacks the right to dispose of the thing. This includes cases in which the alienator was never the owner and cases in which the alienator's right to dispose was annulled retroactively.
Cases in which the right of the alienator was terminated without retroactive effect (through the fulfilment of a resolutive condition or through the exercise of the right of revendication under art. 7:39 BW) are not covered by art. 3:86, as the

[180] The subsidiary protection which art. 3:88 BW may provide, discussed above in § 5.1.3, will not receive any attention here.

acquirer did not acquire from someone who lacked the right to dispose at the time of the transfer: that right was terminated at a later stage.
The bona fide purchase of registered property is covered by art. 3:88 BW; see above, § 5.1.3 for the conditions (rather different from those found in art. 3:86) under which its protection can be invoked.
For several negotiable instruments there are separate provisions: e.g. for bills of exchange art. 115 K, for promissory notes art. 176 K, for cheques art. 198 K. For warehouse warrants (Dutch: *ceel*[181]) a separate provision is lacking, so art. 3:86 is applicable here.
For works of art (cultural objects in the sense of article 1 *under* 1 of Directive No. 93/7/EEC of the Council of the European Communities of 15 March 1993 on the return of cultural objects unlawfully removed from the territory of a Member State (OJEC 1993 L 74) and objects that are protected under the Cultural Heritage Preservation Act (*Wet tot behoud van cultuurbezit*)) special rules are formulated in art. 3:86a BW.[182]

11.2. Acquisition for value

For two reasons, art. 3:86 only protects in the case of acquisition for value. The first reason is fairness: compared to someone who has made a counterperformance, it is less difficult for the donee to have go give up the thing he has acquired a non domino. The fairness argument only applies if the owner of the thing had himself acquired it for value, but the law does not make an exception for cases in which the thing is revendicated by an owner who had acquired it by gratuitous title. The second reason why art. 3:86 requires acquisition for value is the fact that the provision is regarded to entail protection of business and trade (in Dutch: *verkeersbescherming*): in this field the principle of *do ut des* is considered an essential characteristic.[183]
The line between acquisition for value and gratuitous acquisition[184] is not a sharp one. A merely symbolical counterperformance is not sufficient, but, on the other hand, it is not required that the counterperformance has more or less the same value as the acquired object. If the price was e.g. 50% of the value, this could not

---

[181] Art. 7:607 BW.
[182] In short, the rules amount to a limitation of the protection of the bona fide acquirer of these works of art, but under certain circumstances the judge is entitled to award the possessor an equitable remuneration.
[183] See on this subject further A.F. Salomons, "De pijlers onder de vertrouwensbescherming van artikel 3:86 Nieuw BW", *Ars Aequi* 40 (1991) 10, pp. 114-123.
[184] Gratuitous acquisition (in Dutch: *verkrijging om niet*) is usually a gift but this is not necessarily so. E.g. when a possessor acquires ownership because the owner waives his right: this acquisition is also gratuitous but is not a gift; see Snijders/Rank-Berenschot, *Goederenrecht*, p. 297

be called gratuitous either.[185] To be entitled to the protection of art. 3:86, it is not required that the price has already been paid: it is sufficient that the transferor is entitled to a counterperformance.

11.3. Possession/physical control of the "transferor" required?

Art. 3:86 is essentially the codicifation of the case law of the *Hoge Raad* since 1950. In that year, the *Hoge Raad* ruled[186] that the acquirer a non domino in good faith is entitled to protection against the fact that the transferor lacks the right to dispose, but not against the absence of a valid title or the absence of delivery. This ruling (as well as subsequent rulings in which the 1950 decision was confirmed and elaborated) was and is regarded as the acceptance of the ‚legitimation doctrine' (*legitimatieleer*) of the Amsterdam legal scholar Paul Scholten. The basis of this doctrine is that the acquirer a non domino of a movable is entitled to protection because he has relied upon the de facto power of the transferor: that ‚real possession' (*reëel bezit*) legitimizes the transferor as the owner. The physical control of the transferor is therefore a crucial element of the legitimation doctrine, and some authors assume that the absence of physical control is an obstacle to the protection of the acquirer a non domino.[187] This has not been laid down in the new code of 1992, however, and there is no recent case law on this queston either.[188] Most authors therefore assume that the physical control of the transferor is not required.[189]

11.4. Is acquisition of physical control by the acquirer required?

When a movable is delivered by constitutum possessorium, this delivery is without effect with respect to a third person who has a prior right to the thing until the time when the thing has come into the hands of the acquirer, unless the third person has consented to the alienation; see art. 3:90 § 2 BW. This implies that the

---

[185] See Pitlo-Reehuis, *Goederenrecht*, p. 132.

[186] HR 10-5-1950, NJ 1951, 1 (*Damhof/Staat*).

[187] See, for example, O.K. Brahn, „Ons allernieuwste 2014", *WPNR* 5739 (1985), pp. 333-342 (341). See for a discussion and further references A.F. Salomons, „Inpassen of aanpassen? Vermogensrecht voor het digitale tijdperk" , *WPNR* 6427 (2000), pp. 901-907.

[188] The most recent decision of the *Hoge Raad* on this issue is more than 50 years old: in HR 29-2-1952, NJ 1953, 58 (*Drukpersarrest*), the *Hoge Raad* decided that the acquirer should have relied on physical control by the transferor.

[189] See Schut-Rodenburg, *Bescherming van de verkrijger van roerende zaken* (1986), pp. 80-82, W.G. Huijgen, "Vuistpand en vruchtgebruik: onzekere (zekerheids)rechten", *WPNR* 6181 (1995), pp. 323-325 and *WPNR* 6199 (1995), pp. 720-722, and A.F. Salomons, "Inpassen of aanpassen? Vermogensrecht voor het digitale tijdperk" , *WPNR* 6427 (2000), pp. 901-907 (arguing that holding on to the doctrine that the physical control of the transferor is required is unwise in view of the advance of e-commerce: when someone buys via the internet, he has not relied upon any real possession of the transferor, because he is not a witness to that possession).

acquirer a non domino is not saved from revendication by the depossessed owner as long as he leaves the thing in the hands of the transferor or someone on his behalf: the delivery lacks effect with respect to the owner, and therefore the transfer is invalid with respect to the owner: art. 3:86 protects against the absence of the right to dispose, but not against the absence of a valid title or the absence of a valid delivery (see above. § 11.3.).
The effect and ratio of art. 3:90 § 2 has been discussed in more detail above, § 1.2.1., 2.3., 4.1.1. and 5.4.2.a., to which I refer.

11.5. Specific requirements regarding the "transferor"?

A distinction has to be made between the acquisition of a stolen thing and the acquisition of a thing which has not been stolen (lost things are included in this category in view of the fact that the owner usually, at least to some extent, is to blame for the loss, but not for the theft).
If a non-stolen thing is transferred, it is not relevant in which way the transferor was enabled to deliver the thing to the acquirer who invokes art. 3:86; usually embezzlement by a detentor, but it may also be that the transferor had acquired the thing from the owner but at a later stage the title of his transfer was annulled (which leads to a return of ownership with retroactive effect, but not to a return of possession). Another possibility is that the thing had been lost by the owner and was found by the transferor; in that case it depends on his behaviour whether he is to be regarded as a possessor or as a detentor. In any case: in these instances there are no specific requirements regarding the transferor.
This is different if the thing was stolen. In that case, the additional requirements of art. 3:86 § 3 under a have to be met.[190] These requirements are as follows:

A With regard to the acquirer:
- the thing has been acquired by a natural person;
- this aquirer was not acting in the exercise of a profession or business;

B With regard to the transferor:
- he has acquired from an alienator whose business it is to deal with the public in similar things;
- otherwise than at a public sale;
- the alienator was in the ordinary exercise of his business.

[190] This is also the case when the theft was due to gross negligence; see HR 18-1-1991, NJ 1992, 667 (*Centraal Beheer/Gritter*): the owner of a valuable car had left this car unattended for several weeks in the car park of an international airport which was entirely open to the public, while all car registration papers where left in the car. Despite his carelessness, the owner had not lost the right to revendicate the car when it was stolen and transferred to a third person (who was obviously not entitled to invoke the protection of the acquirer a non domino of (the forerunner of) art. 3:86 BW).

C With regard to the place of the transaction or, as the case may be, the place where the business of the transferor is established:

- on business premises destined for that purpose, being an immovable structure or part thereof with the land belonging thereto.

It follows from these requirements that acquisition at a public auction or at a market is excluded. The legislator has tried to balance the need to fight crime (to discourage theft by hampering the trade in stolen goods) against the need to protect those who are dependent on the acquisition of used goods. The outcome of this consideration is to be found in art. 3:86 § 3 under a: protection of the buyer of a stolen movable is possible if he is a consumer, the seller a professional, and the purchase took place in a location where the buyer could not have been aware of the presence of stolen goods. See on the criteria for this protection HR 14-11-1997, NJ 1998, 147 (*Gestolen caravan*).[191]

11.6. Good faith

The acquirer has – at the moment of the acquisition - to be in good faith with regard to the right of the transferor to dispose of the thing. If the issue is taken to court, the acquirer has to state the circumstances which justify that he accepted the transferor as being entitled to dispose and which exclude that he had reason to doubt his right. If these stated circumstances validate an appeal to good faith, the burden of proof of the incorrectness of the buyer's statements rests on the dispossessed owner.[192]

Pursuant to art. 3:11 BW, the acquirer "is not acting in good faith if he knew the facts or the law to which his good faith must relate or if, in the given circumstances, he should know them." This implies a *duty to inquire* into the right of the transferor to dispose, under penalty of not being entitled to invoke art. 3:86 BW, even if it was not possible to start an inquiry: "Impossibility to inquire does not prevent the person, who had good reasons to be in doubt, from being considered as someone who should know the facts or the law" (art. 3:11 last sentence).

As we have just seen, whether or not the acquirer should have known the transferor was not entitled to dispose, is dependent upon the circumstances. Therefore, it is not possible to give a general answer to the question whether only

[191] This case concerned the sale of a stolen caravan. All requirements for the protection of the buyer were met, except for one: there was no immovable structure in which the seller exercised his business. The *Hoge Raad* decided that the buyer could nevertheless invoke art. 3:86 § 3 under a: protection in this case was in accordance with the considerations which had led the legislator to impose the provision, and furthermore on the premises of the seller a movable caravan was at hand which, looking like an immovable structure, served as his sales-office. See on this case A.F. Salomons, "Plaats voor derdenbescherming?", *WPNR* 6298 (1998), pp. 46-48.

[192] *Parl.Gesch.* Boek 3, p. 1214.

actual knowledge and gross negligence or even slight negligence exclude good faith: when someone buys a car at a market which is known to be a place where stolen and embezzled cars are frequently traded, a very thorough inquiry into the right of the transferor is expected. On the other hand, in the case of the purchase of a second-hand book of little value in a antiquarian bookshop with an excellent reputation no such far-reaching inquiries are required. In case law, the duty to inquire is elaborated primarily in the context of car sales.

An additional rule is found in art. 3:87 § 1 BW:[193]

> *An acquirer, who is asked within three years from his acquisition to identify the alienator, must, without delay, provide all information which is necessary to trace that person or which he could have considered as being sufficient for that purpose at the time of his acquisition. If he does not comply with this obligation, he may not invoke the protection which articles 86 and 86a afford to an acquirer in good faith.*

This entails a duty – ending three years after the acquisition - of the acquirer to give the original owner any information needed to trace the transferor. This is an addition to the duty to inquire under art. 3:11 BW. If the acquirer refuses or is unable to give the required information, he is not entitled to invoke art. 3:86. As in the case of art. 3:11, the scope of the duty of art. 3:87 depends upon the circumstances: when someone buys a valuable object from a salesman at the door it is not sufficient merely to rely upon the name and address stated by the salesman, but in the case of a purchase at a regular market the information acquired about the seller may be less detailed.[194] See on the *wegwijsplicht* ("duty to show the way") of art. 3:87 also above, § 5.1.3.

11.7. Is there a right for the original owner to buy back the asset from the good faith acquirer?

When art. 3:86 applies, i.e. when its protection is awarded, the acquirer becomes the owner. This means that the provision functions not merely as a safeguard, a defence against the revendication of the dispossessed owner, but has "real" effect: ownership is transferred despite the absence of the right to dispose on the part of the "second hand" (the transferor).
Authors are divided on the question whether art. 3:86 (as well as the other provisions which award proprietary third party protection, like art. 3:88 and 7:42 BW) has ipso jure effect or its protection should be invoked in order to be awarded. In the latter case, the acquirer a non domino is free to choose whether or not he wants to be protected (at the expense of the former owner), in the former

[193] The second paragraph excludes money from the scope of this rule.
[194] See *Parl.Gesch.* Boek 3, p. 344-346.

case he becomes the owner, whether he likes it or not. The literal text of art. 3:86 indicates that the legislator was of the opinion that the protection should work ipso jure, but the authors who reject this view and favour a system in which third party protection is a competence state that it is not up to the legislator to decide on dogmatic issues like this one. This seems to be the prevailing opinion.[195] A solid argument against this view is that prescription also works ipso facto, and should even be applied by the judge ex officio.[196]

The system described here was enacted in the new civil code of 1992. In the decades in which work on the code was in progress (the commission to draft a new code was awarded in 1947) many different drafts on this issue circulated before the final text of art. 3:86 was decided upon. In the original draft a right was included for the dispossessed owner to buy the movable back from the acquirer a non domino. The first sentence of the first paragraph of the draft-article stated that the acquisition a non domino for value is valid in the case of good faith. The draft-article added:[197]

> *He who, pursuant to the provision of the first sentence of the first paragraph, has lost his right, is entitled within three years afterwards to demand the transfer of the thing by the owner, against remuneration of the damage which the owner suffers by the restitution of the thing. The owner is entitled to set a reasonable term for the demand of restitution.*

This repurchase right (*terugkooprecht*) was not included in the final draft. One of the reasons was that it would probably lead to more court cases than the system that was finally chosen. Furthermore, the legislator preferred a system which was not too different from current law (to enhance support for the implementation of the new code).

11.8. Bona fide purchase free of encumbrances

The problem which arises when someone acquirers a movable, unaware of the fact that it is encumbered with a right of pledge or usufruct of a third person, is solved in the second paragraph of art. 3:86 BW:

> *Where property mentioned in paragraph 1 and having been transferred, otherwise than by gratuitous title and according to articles 90, 91 or 93, is encumbered with a dismembered right which the acquirer does not know nor ought to have known at the time of the transfer, this right is*

[195] See e.g. Asser-Mijnssen-De Haan, *Goederenrecht* § 306 and B.W.M. Nieskens-Isphording and A.E.M. van der Putt-Lauwers, *Derdenbescherming* (3rd ed; Deventer 2002) § 1.6.

[196] See *Parl.Gesch.* Boek 3, pp. 415-416. See for a defence of the view that art. 3:86 works ipso facto further A.F. Salomons, "Recht voor verstrooiden", *J.L.P. Cahen-bundel* (Deventer 1997), pp. 301-312 at 310.

[197] See *Parl.Gesch.* Boek 3, p. 321 ff.

extinguished; in the case of a transfer according to article 91, the extinction is subject to the same suspensive condition as the delivery.

It is irrelevant whether the transfer was performed by someone who was entitled to dispose of it or by someone who was not: in the latter case there is a concurrence of the protection of § 1 (against the dispossessed owner) and that of § 2 (against the pledgeholder or usufructuary).

12. Acquisitive prescription of movable property

12.1. Requirements of acquisitive prescription

According to art. 3:99 BW the period of acquisitive prescription is:

- 3 years in the case of movable things which are not registered property and rights under documents payable to bearer and order (stolen objects are not excluded);[198]
- 10 years for other property.[199]

The prescription starts with the commencement of the day following the beginning of the possession (art. 3:101 BW). The term of acquisition is complete when the last day of the prescribed period has elapsed.
According to art. 3:102 BW, a person who succeeds to the possession of another by *general title* continues an already running prescription, even if he is not in good faith (as the acquirer under general title continues the possession with the same quality and subject to the same defects as that of the predecessors; art. 3:116 BW).
If someone has acquired possession from another person otherwise than by general title, the continuation of a running prescription requires that the possessor is in good faith (art. 3:102 § 2). If the predecessor was not in good faith but the acquirer is, a new prescription period commences at the moment when possession is given to the acquirer.
Prescription requires *possession in good faith.*[200] Whether someone is a possessor has to be determined according to common opinion, taking into account the rules

---

[198] Pursuant to the second paragraph of art. 3:99, this does not apply to movable things which, pursuant to the Cultural Heritage Preservation Act (*Wet tot behoud van cultuurbezit*), have been designated as protected objects, or which form part of a public collection or an inventory list as referred to in Article 14a, paragraph 2, of that Act, provided that possession has commenced after that designation or during the time they formed part of that collection or inventory.
[199] See also *Parl.Gesch.* Boek 3, p. 425: prescription is possible for every patrimonial right which is not entirely personal.
[200] For prescription of a succession, possession during a certain period is insufficient. Art. 3:100 BW provides: *A person who has taken possession of a succession cannot acquire that succession*

of art. 3:109-117 BW, and, otherwise, the facts as they appear. See for an elaboration of this provision of art. 3:108 BW above, § 2.1. The possessor is in good faith if he believes himself to be the title-holder and is reasonably justified in that belief. Once a possessor is in good faith, he is considered to remain so. Good faith is presumed; absence of good faith must be proven (art. 3:118 § 1-3). In art. 3:105 another form of prescription is found, for which good faith is *not* required: this will be discussed below, in § 12.2.
Prescription also requires the possession to be *uninterrupted*. The possessor does not have to prove that his possession was continuous; possession which has begun continues until it is evident that the possessor abandons the property or when another acquires possession of it (irrespective of how this occurred: by taking possession, by transfer of possession, or by succession) (art. 3:117). Interruption or extension of prescription of the right of Action to terminate possession interrupts or extends acquisitive prescription accordingly (art. 3:104). Involuntary loss of property does not interrupt prescription, provided that possession is recovered within a year or an Action instituted within a year leads to such recovery (art. 3:103 BW).

12.2. "Thief becomes owner": limitation with acquisitive effect

Unlike in German law, Dutch law is not familiar with the phenomenon of limitation to the right of ownership (*Verjährung des Eigentums*). However, art. 3:105 BW provides a form of prescription, the effects of which bear similarities to limitation of ownership. Art. 3:105 § 1 reads as follows:

> *A person who possesses property at the time of the completion of the prescription of the right of Action to terminate possession, acquires the property even if his possession was not in good faith.*

This provision has already been mentioned above, in § 2.2 under 3.2. Its effect is commonly referred to by the slogan "thief becomes owner": a thief who succeeds in hiding his loot for twenty years[201] acquires ownership and can no longer be held accountable (neither in civil nor in penal law).[202] The hiding of the loot may constitute a separate unlawful act, but this offers no solution as the right of Action to end the unlawful hiding of the loot is prescribed simultaneous with the

---

by prescription nor the property belonging to it to the detriment of the title-holder until after the latter's Action to claim that succession has been prescribed.

[201] See art. 3:306 BW: *Unless otherwise provided for by law, the prescription period for rights of Action is twenty years.*

[202] See for a discussion on the merits of art. 3:105 e.g. C.J.H. Brunner, "Dief wordt eigenaar", in: *Quod Licet (KLeijn-bundel)* (Deventer 1992), pp. 45-53.; R.J.Q. Klomp, "Dieven met geduld. Over verkrijgende verjaring te kwader trouw", in: *Tijd en onzekerheid. BW-krant Jaarboek* 16 (Deventer 2000), pp. 59-73, and P. Neleman, "Thieves' paradise revisited", *Brunner-bundel* (Deventer 1994), pp. 293-302.

prescription of the revendication. The same applies mutatis mutandis to the prescrip tion of the right of Action to terminate the possession of the thief on the basis of the fact that he is not the title-holder of the property. See art. 3:314 BW:

1 *The prescription period of a right of Action to terminate an unlawful situation begins to run at the beginning of the day following the one on which the immediate termination of that situation can be claimed.*

2 *The prescription period of a right of Action to terminate the possession of a non-title-holder begins to run at the beginning of the day following the one on which the non-title-holder has become possessor or on which the immediate termination of the situation of which his possession forms the continuation could be claimed.*

The acquisition of art. 3:105 takes place on behalf of the actual possessor, irrespective of how long his possession has lasted and irrespective of whether his possession was interrupted or not. If the property was encumbered with a restricted right, this right remains valid until the right of Action of the title-holder of that restricted right prescribes.[203]

13. Reservation of title

A reservation of title (in Dutch: *eigendomsvoorbehoud*) is a stipulation in the title of transfer of a movable thing to the effect that ownership of that thing, despite delivery thereof, is reserved by the transferor, until a performance is made by the acquirer.[204] When such a stipulation is included in a contract, the transferor is presumed to obligate himself to the transfer of the thing to the acquirer under a suspensive condition of performance; art. 3:92 BW.[205] The delivery of a movable thing which is unregistered property and which is under the control of the alienator in the performance of an obligation to transfer under suspensive condition is accomplished by giving the acquirer control over the thing; art. 3:91 BW. The proprietary consequence of a transfer under such a condition is found in art. 3:84 § 4: Where delivery is made in the performance of a conditional obligation, the right so acquired is subject to the same condition as the obligation. This implies that the transition of ownership is postponed until the fulfilment of the condition.

---

[203] See *Parl.Gesch.* Boek 3, p. 417.

[204] See E.B. Rank-Berenschot, *Tekst en commentaar Burgerlijk Wetboek*, note 1 ad art. 3:92 BW.

[205] Art. 3:92 entails no more than a legal presumption: other constructions to the effect of a reservation of title may also be valid.

13.1. Ownership or security right?

As long as the performance by the acquirer remains unfulfilled, ownership remains with the transferor. This retained ownership is susceptible to transfer to another person (see HR 28-4-1989, NJ 1990, 252 (*Puinbreekinstallatie*)). That the retained right really is ownership and not merely a security right like a pledge is also shown by the fact that it is not a dependent right (see art. 3:7 BW) nor an accessory right (see art. 6:142-144 BW),[206] and by the fact that there are no formal requirements like a written document or registration to make the title reservation effective in relation to third parties. In the case of non-performance on the part of the buyer the seller is not obliged to levy execution and take recourse, as a pledgeholder or a mortgagee would be: the prohibition on appropriation (art. 3:235 BW) applies to a pledge or hypothec, but not to reservation of title.
On the other hand, the reservation of title is regarded and treated as a right that predominantly serves as a security right by the treasury. When the tax authorities exercise their right of seizure (in Dutch: *fiscaal bodemrecht)* it spares the property rights of third parties, provided that they are considered "real property" (*reële eigendom*). Things which had been given to the taxpayer on loan, in custody or in operation lease are considered real property of the lender, the depositor and the lessor respectively, but this does not apply in the case of reservation of title, hire-purchase or financial lease. In other words, the seller would have to tolerate that the treasury seizes and levies execution of the goods which were transferred under title reservation. In this, a security right feature manifests itself, and therefore one has to conclude that the title reservation has a hybrid nature: ownership *and* a security right.[207]

13.2. For which claims?

Pursuant to art. 3:92 § 2, a reservation of title may only be validly stipulated with respect to:

- claims concerning the counterperformance for things delivered or to be delivered by the alienator to the acquirer pursuant to a contract;
- claims for work performed or to be performed pursuant to such a contract for the benefit of the acquirer;
- claims for failure to perform such contracts.

To the extent that a condition is void upon this ground, it is held to be unwritten. This implies that the contract in itself remains valid, and only the stipulation is disregarded.

---

[206] *Parl.Gesch.* Boek 3, p. 1241-1242.
[207] Snijnders/Rank-Berenschot, *Goederenrecht*, no. 498.

13.3. The tranferor's and acquirer's right to dispose

If the transferor who stipulated a reservation of title lacked the right to dispose of the thing, the acquirer is in need of recourse to the protection which art. 3:86 awards to the bona fide acquirer a non domino (see above, section 11). In order to be entitled to that protection, he needs to be in good faith at the moment of delivery, i.e. the moment he was given control over the thing (art. 3:91). It is not required that his good faith continues until the fulfilment of the suspensive condition.[208]
If the acquirer transfers the thing to a third person before the condition is fulfilled (i.e. before his performance to the first transferor), he is disposing of the property of the transferor. The validity of the second transfer depends on the answer to the question whether he had the right to dispose of the property. This would be the case when the first transferor had explicitly conferred him with this right contractually (*geclausuleerd eigendomsvoorbehoud*). Another possibility is that it can be deduced from the contract between the first transferor and the acquirer that the latter was entitled to dispose of the detained property; nevertheless it is not sufficient that the property was destined to be resold.[209] If neither is the case, this acquirer, too, needs the protection of the bona fide acquirer a non domino. The mere fact that he might have realised that the thing was 'encumbered' with a reservation of title is insufficient to deprive him of good faith: he must have been entitled to assume that the transferor had the right to transfer the thing, regardless of any reservation of title. This will for example be the case when a normal business transaction is concluded and the acquirer had no reason to expect the exercise of the reservation of title. A similar rule applies when a movable thing is reclaimed by the seller of a movable thing under his right of revendication (*reclamerecht*) and the thing has already been resold: the third acquirer is protected by art. 7:42 BW, provided he acquired the thing for value and he could not reasonably expect that the seller would exercise his right of revendication. The solution is also in accordance with established case law.[210]

---

[208] See Pitlo-Reehuis, *Goederenrecht*, p. 680.

[209] This was decided in HR 14-2-1992, NJ 1993, 623 (*Love-Love*) concerning the sale of the hull of a ship which was transferred under reservation of title by a shipbuilder to another shipbuilder, who was to finish the ship and market it. The mere fact that the ship was destined to be resold to a customer did not imply that the second shipbuilder was entitled to dispose of it before completing his performance towards the first shipbuilder.

[210] See HR 6-1-1961, NJ 1962, 19 (*Seneca/Forum*), HR 12-6-1970, NJ 1971, 203 (*Philippens/Omsa*) and HR 29-6-1979, NJ 1980, 133 (*Hoogovens/Matex*): mere knowledge of the existence of a right of retention does not imply the absence of good faith.

13.4. Extended reservation of title

As we have seen, art. 3:92 § 2 enables the stipulation of a reservation of title for certain claims other than the counterprestation for the transferred thing itself; this implies that a *horizontal extension* of the reservation of title is allowed (at least for the claims mentioned in § 2).[211]

Vertical extenstion of the reservation of title, however, is not possible; there is no room to stipulate that the reservation of title also applies to things other than the things which were delivered. This implies that the reservation of title ends when these things are used in a production process and cease to exist due to accession, confusion or specification: it is common opinion that the mandatory legal provisions on original acquisition (art. 5:14-16, see section 10) cannot be thwarted by way of contract.[212] An alternative could be the stipulation of a silent pledge in advance with regard to the things which the acquirer will produce (but it may well be that the acquirer had at an earlier stage pledged all his present and future goods in advance to his bank, and in that case the pledge of the seller is subordinated to that of the bank).

13.5. Extinction of the title reservation

The most important ways in which the reserved ownership would end, are the following:[213]

- The acquirer performs, which implies the fulfilment of the suspensive condition and ipso facto transition of ownership to the acquirer. Pursuant to art. 3:92 § 3 BW, the condition is deemed to be fulfilled when the alienator receives satisfaction otherwise than by performance of the counterprestation, when the acquirer is relieved of his obligation to perform pursuant to article 6:60 BW,[214] and when the prescription of the right of Action in respect of the counterprestation has been completed. In the absence of a stipulation to the contrary, the same applies in the event of the abandonment of the right to the counterprestation.
- The acquirer transfers the thing to a third party (assuming he had the right to dispose thereof, see above).

---

[211] See Snijnders/Rank-Berenschot, *Goederenrecht*, no. 490.

[212] See Pitlo-Reehuis, *Goederenrecht*, pp. 683-694 and Snijnders/Rank-Berenschot, *Goederenrecht*, no. 500.

[213] See Snijnders/Rank-Berenschot, *Goederenrecht*, no. 500 and Pitlo-Reehuis, *Goederenrecht*, pp. 687-688.

[214] Art. 6:60 BW: ***Where the creditor is in default, the judge may discharge the debtor, upon his demand, from his obligation, with or without conditions to be determined by the judge.***

- The acquirer delivers the thing to a third party despite the fact that he lacks the right to dispose thereof, but the third party successfully invokes the protection of the bona fide acquirer a non domino (art. 3:86 BW).
- The thing ceases to exist due to accession, confusion or specification and the applicable rule does not award ownership or co-ownership to the transferor (see art. 5:14-16 and section 10).
- The thing is lost etc. In that case, no substitution of property takes place, even though such a substitution of property does take place in the case of a pledge or hypothec; see art. 3:229: *The right of pledge or hypothec entails a ipso facto right of pledge upon all claims for compensation which take the place of the pledged or hypothecated property, including claims resulting from its depreciation.* This applies to insurance payments, claims by reason of overdistribution, unlawful acts, decrease in value of the thing, expropriation etc. The claim with respect to the payment of the purchase price does not constitute a claim for compensation as meant in art. 3:229.[215]

[215] See W.G. Huijgen, *Tekst en Commentaar Nieuw Burgerlijk Wetboek*, note 1 ad art. 3:229.

Part IV. Additional questions

14. Unspecified goods

Above, in § 5.6., the principle of individualization has already been mentioned. The principle entails that property which has not been individualized is not susceptible to possession, detention or ownership.[216] This implies that one cannot own a part ("100 litres" or "one quarter") of a non-divided whole (oil tank, shipload etc.), notwithstanding the fact that it is possible to have a *personal* right to the delivery of such a part. Generally speaking, it is not possible to own things which are only specified by kind or quantity: only after they are individualized do they become susceptible to ownership.

The same principle is manifested in the rule that "at the title the property to be transferred must be described in a sufficiently precise manner" (art. 3:84 § 2 BW). The *Hoge Raad* has interpreted this rule so, that the individualization must have taken place at the latest at the moment of delivery (i.e. the conclusion of the real agreement), and not, as the text of the provision suggests, at the time of the coming into existence of the title of transfer (usually the conclusion of the obligatory agreement).[217] In other words: when buying bread in a bakery, at the time of the sale the description "one wholewheat bread" is sufficient, but at the time of the delivery it must be established which of the wholewheat breads present in the store is going to be transferred.

With regard to movables,[218] the law of property recognises no provisions that derogate from the system described above. If, for example, a thing that belongs to A is placed in the midst of other, similar things belonging to B, A would not lose his right of ownership on his thing, but, on the other hand, he would not be

---

[216] See Snijders/Rank-Berenschot, *Goederenrecht*, nos. 80, 157 and 161.

[217] See HR 14-10-1994, NJ 1995, 447 (*Spaarbank Rivierenland*).

[218] The last decade has seen a great deal of case law on the question of which role the principle of indivudialization plays in the assignment of claims: to what extent is a detailed description of the claims required in the deed of assignment (art. 3:94 BW). The *Hoge Raad* decided in HR 14-10-1994, NJ 1994, 447 (*Spaarbank Rivierenland*) that it is not necessary to enumerate details like the name of the debtor, the amount of the claim, invoice number, client number etc. It suffices that the deed contains such details that, *if necessary afterwards*, with the help of the deed it can be determined which claims were meant. The deed may, for example, refer to a computer list on which details with regard to the assigned claims are specified. Registration of this computer list is not required. This was confirmed in HR 16-6-1995, NJ 1996, 508 (*Ontvanger/Rabobank IJmuiden*), HR 20-6-1997, NJ 1998, 362 (*Wagemakers q.q./Rabobank Roosendaal*), HR 19-9-1997, NJ 1998, 689 (*Verhagen q.q./IBN II*), HR 19-12-1997 and in NJ 1998, 690 (*Zuidgeest/Furness*). The *Hoge Raad* obviously deems these decisions not to be in conflict with the requirement that "at the title the property to be transferred must be described in a sufficiently precise manner" under art. 3:84 § 2, even though a description of the claims may take place *after* the assignment, i.e. at the moment when the computer list is drawn up. See on this subject e.g. Pitlo-Reehuis, *Goederenrecht* no. 261.

entitled to revendicate it because he is unable to prove which thing is his. This problem of individualisation, therefore, does not belong to the field of property law, but to that of the law of evidence; see above, § 10.3., on 'improper confusion'.

15. Community property

15.1. Sedis materiae

Title 3.7 BW, called "community" (in Dutch: *gemeenschap*), regulates the *proprietary* relationship between the partners in a community (in Dutch: *deelgenoten*[219]). The obligatory relationship between the partners is provided for elsewhere in the BW and can be left aside here.

Title 3.7 of the third Book of the BW is divided into three sections. The first section (art. 3:166-188) provides general provisions, the second (art. 3: 189-194) provides for some special communities and the third (art. 3:195-200) regulates void and annullable partitions.

An important limitation on the scope of title 3.7 is found in art. 3:189 § 1: the provisions of this title do not apply to a marital community, a partnership, a commercial partnership or a shipping partnership, as long as they have not been dissolved; they do not apply either to the community of a building divided into apartment rights, as long as the division has not been terminated. Nevertheless, pursuant to the second paragraph of art. 3:189 the provisions of section 3.7.2 („Some special communities") as well as the provisions of the first section, to the extent that this section does not deviate therefrom, apply to the community of a succession, to a dissolved marital community, partnership, commercial partnership or shipping partnership, and to the community of a building the division of which into apartment rights has been terminated.

From the above it may be deduced that title 3.7 applies primarily to communities which are susceptible to division (commonly referred to as „simple communities", in Dutch: *eenvoudige gemeenschappen*) and not for ‚active' communities which are meant to continue (the „special communities", *bijzondere gemeenschappen*, of section 3.7.2).[220]

---

[219] The notion of co-ownership is reserved to the community with regard to things, i.e. corporeal objects, susceptible to human control.

[220] See Pitlo-Reehuis, *Goederenrecht* , p. 321 and Snijders/Rank-Berenschot, *Goederenrecht*, p. 166.

15.2. Communities; classification

A classification of the various communities can be done by several criteria: [221]

- *subject* (e.g. marriage or business);
- *applicable law:* this refers to the following distinction (art. 3:189):
  - 'special' communities;
  - 'simple' communities, which occur in two forms:
    - community of one good (e.g. a common wall);
    - community comprising several goods.[222]
- *origin:*
  - act of formation (e.g. contract, as in the case of a partnership contract in Dutch: *maatschapscontract*);
  - last will and testament (see art. 4:921 BW);
  - the law itself (e.g. in the case of accession or specification if there are no principal thing and component parts the owners of the original things are the co-owners of the new thing; art. 3:15-16 BW).

As has been said above, the provisions of section 3.7.1 apply in principle to all these communities, but an exception is made for those communities which are meant to continue: these are governed by their own rules (e.g. for the not yet dissolved marital community articles 1:93 ff. BW).

15.3. Community; the right to dispose[223]

Only the partners acting together are entitled to dispose of *a good of the community*.. There is an exception to this rule if one of the partners is entitled to dispose of the property because:

- he has the authorisation of the court to do so (art. 3:174);
- because the rules regulating their relationship entitle him to perform the management of the property, and the transfer of the common good could be regarded as such (art. 3:170 § 2);

---

[221] This survey is for the greatest part derived from Snijders/Rank-Berenschot, *Goederenrecht*, p. 168 and Jac. Hijma/M.M. Olthof, *Compendium van het Nederlands vermogensrecht* (8th ed., Deventer 2002), no. 197.

[222] The occurance of the latter kind of community is the result either of the connection between the goods, e.g. a flock of sheep, or of the legal relationship between the partners); otherwise, there is a separate community with regard to each individual good; see Hijma/ Olthof, *Compendium*, no. 197.

[223] See especially Hijma/ Olthof, *Compendium*, no. 199 and Hartkamp, *Compendium*, nos. 145-146.

- because the transfer constitutes an act for the purpose of ordinary maintenance or preservation of common property or, generally, as an act which cannot be postponed; these acts may be performed by any one of the partners, if necessary independently of the others (art. 3:170 § 1).

With regard to the *right to dispose of shares*, one has to distinguish between:

- The right to dispose of an *undivided share in a separate good of the community.*[224] A further distinction has to be made with regard to:
    - *'simple community';* each of the partners is entitled to dispose, unless the juridical relationship between the partners produces a different result (art. 3:175 § 1);[225]
    - *'special community':* the partner may not separately dispose of his share in property belonging to the community (art. 3:190 § 1 and 2).[226]
- The right to dispose of an *undivided share in the totality of the community.*

Unless the juridical relationship between the partners produces a different result, each of the partners is entitled separately. With regard to the 'simple' community, this can be deduced from art. 3:175 § 1 BW,[227] with regard to the 'special' community, see art. 3:191 § 1 BW.[228]

---

[224] *Delivery* of a share in property is made analogously to delivery of that property and has analogous effects; art. 3:96 BW. Therefore, the delivery of a share in a movable thing is performed by the giving of possession of the share (art. 3:96 ° 90). When the transferor lacks the right to dispose of the share, the acquirer has recourse to the protection of the bone fide acquirer a non domino of art. 3:86 (because the delivery of the share in the property has "analogous effects" of the delivery of that property): see on the complications the transfer of co-ownership of a movable thing through the giving of co-possession HR 28-4-1989, NJ 1990, 252 (*Puinbreekinstallatie*). See Pitlo-Reehuis, *Goederenrecht*, no. 295.

[225] § 3 adds: *Creditors may seize and execute against the share of a partner in common property. After seizure and execution against a share, limitations on the power to dispose of the shares cannot be invoked between the acquirer of such a share and the remaining partners.*

[226] And his creditors may not seize and execute against such a share, without the consent of the other partners. Nevertheless, a partner can establish a right of pledge or of hypothec upon such a share, even without the consent of the other partners. Unless the other partners consent, the pledgee and the hypothecary creditor may not proceed to the sale of the property as long as it belongs to the community. The difference between the simple and the special community in this respect is easily explained: the latter form of community is meant for continued existance, whereas the simple community is (already) susceptible to division; see Snijders/Rank-Berenschot, *Goederenrecht* p. 175.

[227] Each partner is entitled to dispose of his share in separate goods of the simple community, which may consist of several goods: this implies that he may also dispose of his share in the entire community. See e.g. A.S. Hartkamp, *Compendium*, no. 146.

[228] This provision adds that the creditors of a partner can seize and execute against such a share.

Salzburger Studien zum Europäischen Privatrecht

Herausgegeben von J. Michael Rainer

Band 1 Marc Herzog: Die Haftung des Gastwirts für eingebrachte Sachen des Gasts nach §§ 701 - 703 des Deutschen Bürgerlichen Gesetzbuchs. 1999.

Band 2 Andreas Reinhart: Familienplanungsschaden. Wrongful birth, wrongful life, wrongful conception, wrongful pregnancy. Eine rechtsvergleichende Untersuchung anhand des deutschen und des anglo-amerikanischen Rechts. 1999.

Band 3 Markus Frank: Untersuchungen zu den *Politika* des Aristoteles. 1999.

Band 4 Stefan Josef Schermaier: Der Gemeinschaftsrechtliche Staatshaftungsanspruch. Entwicklung, Perspektiven und Auswirkungen auf das österreichische Recht. 1999.

Band 5 Carmen Windhaber: Reiserecht in Österreich, Deutschland und Kanada. 2000.

Band 6 Korbinian Dietl: Unfallhaftung beim Expeditions- und Trekkingbergsteigen. Zugleich ein Beitrag zum Reiserecht für den Bereich der Bergreisen sowie zum Sporthaftungsrecht für den Bereich des Bergsports. 2000.

Band 7 Erich Jeroscheg: Eigentum an beweglichen Sachen. Französisches Recht und Rechtsvergleich. 2000.

Band 8 Thomas Tschaler: Das Moment der Gefahr als Element der Schadenszurechnung im System des Haftpflichtrechts. Eine rechtstheoretische Untersuchung der möglichen Schwächen gängiger Haftungsmodelle. 2000.

Band 9 Christian Hellenthal: Zulässigkeit einer supranationalen Fußball-Europaliga nach den Bestimmungen des europäischen Wettbewerbsrechts. 2000.

Band 10 Wolfgang Bengen: Die Systematik des § 823 I BGB im Deliktsrecht. Zugleich ein Beitrag zu den Verkehrspflichten. 2000.

Band 11 Gerhard Pöttler: Vergleichende Verbraucherschutzrichtlinienumsetzung in europäischen Mitgliedsstaaten. Anhand ausgewählter Beispiele der Pauschalreise-, Timesharing- und Produkthaftungsrichtlinie. 2001.

Band 12 Johannes Michael Rainer: Europäisches Privatrecht. Die Rechtsvergleichung. 2002.

Band 13 Erwin Schön: Allgemeines Vertragsrecht und Kaufvertragsrecht - ein Rechtsvergleich Österreich, USA, Spanien und UN-Kaufrecht. Unter Einbeziehung von PECL und UNIDROIT-Prinzipien. Gemeinsamkeiten, Unterschiede, Bewertungsversuche. 2003.

Band 14 Patrick Schenner: Skiunfall! Wer haftet? Schadenersatz im österreichischen Skirecht. 2003.

Band 15 Peter Unterkofler: Die rechtliche Stellung des Pflichtteilsberechtigten im Spannungsverhältnis zwischen Erbrecht und Privatstiftungsrecht. 2003.

Band 16 Susanne Spaun: Der Herausgabeanspruch bei Diebstahl oder illegalem Export von Kulturgütern. 2003.

Band 17 Josef Wolff: Trust, Fiducia und fiduziarische Treuhand. Historisch-rechtsvergleichende Untersuchung mit einer Darstellung des Trust in Schottland sowie des römischen und österreichischen Fideikommiss. 2005.

Band 18 Johannes Michael Rainer / Johanna Filip-Fröschl: Transfer of Title Concerning Movables Part I – Eigentumsübertragung an beweglichen Sachen in Europa Teil I. Introduction, Estonia, Italy, Poland, Portugal, Scotland, Slovenia. Einführung, Estland, Italien, Polen, Portugal, Schottland, Slowenien. Edited by Johannes Michael Rainer – Herausgegeben von Johannes Michael Rainer. 2006.

Band 19 Mary-Rose McGuire: Transfer of Title Concerning Movables Part II – Eigentumsübertragung an beweglichen Sachen in Europa Teil II. National Report: Germany. Edited by Johannes Michael Rainer – Herausgegeben von Johannes Michael Rainer. 2006.

Band 20 Claes Martinson: Transfer of Title Concerning Movables Part III – Eigentumsübertragung an beweglichen Sachen in Europa Teil III. National Report: Sweden. Edited by Johannes Michael Rainer – Herausgegeben von Johannes Michael Rainer. 2006.

Band 21 Arthur Salomons: Transfer of Title Concerning Movables Part IV – Eigentumsübertragung an beweglichen Sachen in Europa Teil IV. National Report: The Netherlands. Edited by Johannes Michael Rainer – Herausgegeben von Johannes Michael Rainer. 2006.

www.peterlang.de

FSC
www.fsc.org
MIX
Papier | Fördert gute Waldnutzung
FSC® C083411

Kolibri 360 GmbH
Ferdinand-Jühlke-Straße 7
99095 Erfurt, Deutschland
produktsicherheit@kolibri360.de

Druck:
CPI Druckdienstleistungen GmbH
im Auftrag der
Kolibri 360 GmbH
Ferdinand-Jühlke-Str. 7
99095 Erfurt